THE AUTHOR

On both sides of the Atlantic V.S. Pritchett has been acclaimed as one of the great masters of the short story. He is also distinguished as a critic and a traveller. Born in Suffolk in 1900, he left school at the age of sixteen to work in the leather trade in London. In the Twenties in Paris he worked as a shop assistant and as a shellac salesman, and took to journalism, first during the Irish Civil War and later in Spain.

His first book, *Marching Spain*, the account of a long walk from Badajoz to Vigo, was published in 1928 and since then travel has been his recreation, inspiring evocations of places and peoples in *The Spanish Temper* (1954) and *London Perceived* (1962), both published by The Hogarth Press, *Foreign Faces* (1964), *New York Proclaimed* (1965) and *Dublin* (1967). The author of biographies of Balzac and Turgenev, he gave the Clark Lectures on George Meredith in 1969. He was for many years a director of and contributor to the *New Statesman*. He contributes regularly to the *New Yorker* and the *New York Review of Books*. His critical works include *The Living Novel* (1949), *The Myth Makers* (1979), *The Tale Bearers* (1980) and *A Man of Letters* (1985). His two volumes of autobiography, *A Cab at the Door* (1968) and *Midnight Oil* (1971), are well known in Great Britain and abroad. His novels include *Nothing Like Leather* (1935), *Dead Man Leading* (1949) and *Mr Beluncle* (1959). The first volume of his *Collected Stories* appeared in 1982 and *More Collected Stories* in 1983. V.S. Pritchett is married and lives in London.

MARCHING SPAIN

V. S. Pritchett

*New Introduction by
the Author*

THE HOGARTH PRESS

LONDON

To Dorothy

Published in 1988 by
The Hogarth Press
30 Bedford Square, London WC1B 3RP

First published in Great Britain by Ernest Benn Ltd 1928
Copyright © V.S. Pritchett 1928
Introduction copyright © V.S. Pritchett 1988

A CIP catalogue record for this book is available from the British Library.

ISBN 0 7012 0824 4

Printed in Finland by
Werner Söderström Oy

INTRODUCTION

Marching Spain was my first book. It was written in 1927 and was published in 1928, on condition that I finished a collection of short stories and a novel, and it did not earn its advance of £25. I was temporarily driven to earn a living by translating long French and Spanish commercial documents for a Greek at the rate of a farthing a word.

Now, when I re-read my first book, I forgive myself for the patches of rhetorical writing. After all, I reflect, the famous foot-sloggers, like Hazlitt, Stevenson, Meredith, not to mention the poets of the Open Road school, had always harangued the scenery and the people they met as they clumped along, talking and even declaiming to themselves. My own model was the oratorical Hilaire Belloc of *The Path to Rome:* he certainly *marched* for he had done his military service in the French army. I had done no more than to walk through the West of Ireland during the Civil War and once from Paris to Orleans in the belief that this was the only way to know the common people of any country.

I must confess that I knew Spain much better than I pretended. In 1924 after being an untrained reporter in Ireland during the Civil War for the *Christian Science Monitor*, I was sent to Spain during the dictatorship of Primo de Rivera when the censorship made news scarce. Spain became my private university. I settled down to learn Spanish and was soon deep in contemporary Spanish literature, in the essays of Azorin, in the company of Pio Baroja, the conversation of the novelist Perez de Ayala who later became the Spanish Ambassador in London. Unamuno's *The Tragic Sense of Life* became my Bible.

My job came to an end but I returned to Spain almost at

once to do this long walk. The one region I had not seen was the little-visited province close to the Portuguese frontier, known as Las Hurdes, a lonely region of great poverty. In no time in my life except thirty years later when I walked among the primitive poor whites of the Appalachians in the United States have I been so tenderly treated.

When *Marching Spain* was published it was reviewed (I was cheered to see at enormous length) by that great comic writer Beachcomber, famous for *his* long walks in the Pyrenees. He ridiculed my prose and made fun of my attitudinising. On the other hand Desmond MacCarthy's highbrow *Life and Letters* said that if I was crankish I had a good ear, was well-informed and that George Borrow and Richard Ford would gladly make room for me at their table at the Spanish Inn where we would talk of those *cosas de España* - things that can happen only in Spain. Even now I can still hear the lamenting voice of the poor ragged woman riding on a donkey which was led by her two little children, calling out to me at a deserted cross road: 'Sir, I am blind and I cannot see the signpost. The road to Zamora, sir. Tell us the road. God have pity on us. Three leagues riding, sir. A terrible thing it is not to have one's sight.'

One of those *cosas*.

Spain haunted me, until thirty years later I wrote *The Spanish Temper*.

V.S. Pritchett, London 1988

Preface

A strange country draws from the heart strange cries, strange assertions, the fitness and worth of which time alone can test. In my march across Spain from Badajoz to Leon, which this book describes, I have recorded only what then I heard from the people, from the land's voice, and from my own heart. I thought at the time the things that I have set down were significant—does not the present always seem so and oneself the most significant being in it?—and now I try to catch your sympathy, for without it these poor, honest things may appear as empty as a road that has been travelled on in days that cannot come back.

Portions of this book have appeared in
The Manchester Guardian, *The Outlook*,
and *The Christian Science Monitor*

Contents

xi

CHAPTER I

'TO SPAIN AND THE WORLD'S SIDE'

My dreams were of repeated and frustrated attempts at departure. I was in the taxi but the taxi would not go to the station. I was in the station but there was no train. I was in the train but dressed only in pyjamas. I woke up at five o'clock, at half-past five, at twenty-five minutes to six, at twenty to six, at five to six. It was barely light, but I could hear the rubbery shudder of vermilion busses in Tottenham Court Road. I was counting the busses. There were three, four, five, six, but never seven. The seventh bus never came. I had to begin all over again—two, three, four, five, six. At last a bus stopped outside a furniture shop which had a lacquer grandfather clock in the window. *She* was driving the bus. She climbed down from the seat and shouted in my face something about ' Don Quixote,' and I began to remember with embarrassment that I had not read all of the book, but it was impossible to explain that to her and to tell her one is never so heroic as one dreams . . .

Waking, I saw her sitting up in bed, and heard her saying it was seven o'clock and a dull morning.

' Seven,' she said, pushing me.

The dreams and noises went pittering round my head and out of it like mice out of a room at the click of light. I got out of bed and shot the blind up. The cord snapped round and round in a vicious tangle. The prospect of slate roofs, skylights, and backyards was dingy and grey. The morning sky was horn yellow, flat as lead. I looked at the sink, the gas ring, the newspaper bought with lively excitement the day before and now fallen loosely on the floor, the brief flood of adventure ebbed out of the print, her clothes in a little round heap on the chair.

' I can't go,' I said miserably.

The prospect of this long journey to Western Spain and across it, alone and on foot, was horrible. I ached for the heavens to make a sign that would prevent my going. There was no sign. That there should appear a sign in the heavens must be the old desire of baffled, tortured man. I lit the gas and put the kettle on ; went downstairs into the street for the milk. The routine air, neither hot nor cold, smelled of London morning ; yellow, wearied air passing from mouth to mouth. I could hear the tapping heels of factory girls hurrying early to their machines.

' I shan't go,' I said again, but I made the tea and put the last things into my haversack. Books—I hesitated between 'Don Quixote' and 'Tristram Shandy,' and chose the latter because I knew I should never read it. I had long lost all my sentimental illusions about the joys of the open road with a ' beloved classic ' in one's pocket. I gathered together the maps.

We ate our breakfast in silence, she and I. We went out to the tube, walking almost angrily. There was a lawn of daffodils, the double-cassocked ones, risen lyrically in yellow choir, behind the railings of a park ; and two black-pronged trees dipped in a vivid spring paint of buds. At the station stood a man holding a tray of laces and matches, a human shop. We are all shops. I supposed, as we were sucked into the tube, I was going to sell Spain. Down those white pipes we followed the backs of people. At last we were following a man with a folding, red neck. We followed him for miles gratefully. A sign ? A pillar of neck by day ? I longed for the security of a wide, red neck with folds.

A train fell screaming to rest beside us. We got in. We bombarded our way through three or four stations with all the crushing tons of London bearing upon us. We carved beneath it, drilled a trajectory like a fantastic shell, howling and gyrating through space. It was amazing in this shriek of melodrama to see the red necked man sitting opposite us. His face, set in that London glumness, was as smooth and red as his neck, and in his square head, under a slight steam of yellow eyebrow, were eyes as shrewd as two pips. He had a small Gladstone bag at his side. He looked as though he had never been out of a job, an indispensable man putting money by every week ; and he watched me and my suitcase with a perman-ent sniff of disapproval. He was thinking, ' Young fool wasting his money gallivanting about '—he was fond of that word ' gallivanting,' I was sure—' What he wants is a job.'

He got out at Waterloo as well. At Waterloo my green train boiled in and a score of porters rose out of that white lake of asphalt like a flight of ducks to meet it. The platform became troubled with people, and trolleys of luggage buzzed among them like laden bumble bees. I searched the boat train for an empty compartment—the soul's instinctive search for solitude—but the best I could find was a compartment near the engine with a bag on the rack over one corner, indicating one passenger at least.

We sat together in the waiting train for a long time, she and I. Men began to shout on the platform. Luggage charged by like artillery.

' Five to nine,' I said.

' Another five minutes,' she said.

I remembered suddenly I had not given her the keys.

There was a fusillade of banging doors. A man in stained overalls, face livid and tight as steel, walked up the next track bearing an oil can, and Big Ben watched him. One, two, three, four—the great clock spoke out slowly like a grey friar intoning ritual prayers—five, six, seven, eight, nine, an aged voice deadened by the habit of its own wisdom. The man bearing the oil can stood back from the points to avoid the train, looking up with the set lustre of the rails in his face. With a boyish call the train crunched out of the station, puff by puff, thought by thought, with a bell clangour of spinning wheels. Now I saw her eyes shining, dimming, her purple coat stood out for a second, receded, and there was an arm stretched out, a handkerchief that fluttered up and lost itself in a score of handkerchiefs beating, crying like white birds, a confused drizzle of persons disappearing at the curve of the platform, and the station for a moment a pit of tears. I could count every bitter girder of it. She had gone.

The train flowed over a strident river of metals, and some lines we gathered together under our wheels and others we threw aside in armfuls with a crash into the main stream. We were pulled past signal-boxes glittering and crying with alarm. We slid up and down against another train. There were men and women talking together in the other train ; now we were shoulder to shoulder, now a point flung us widely apart. I thought of *her* walking up Tottenham Court Road, where the vibrant buses drummed in vermilion up and down, going into that room again.

The train settled down to its long Alexandrine roll, that gentle iambic variation, the expected upbeat, the elegiac monody of the wheels. For the enjoyment of a faintly literary melancholy there is no place like a train. One sits back, effortlessly casting away the tired landscape of an undesired world. Every sight is succulent food for bitterness : those suburbs like trenches with the wireless entanglements above them, the pillar boxes, the concrete, the sap heads of red London angling into the green country, the jab of a builder's advertisement, some creamy-domed cinema, eight municipal trees. Beauty one wipes out of the mind before it can soak there and stain all, as one wipes tears from the eyes ; but the ugly things, what a vicious pleasure they give, for they enhance the exquisite bitterness of one's loneliness.

I took out the maps. I was travelling to Southampton. From Southampton I was to take the boat first to Vigo, where I should put my suitcase ashore and,

continuing then—still by boat—to Lisbon. From
Lisbon I should take the train to Badajoz on the
Spanish frontier and thence walk northward across
Spain through wide Extremadura—there are leagues
in the name alone—over the low spur of the Gredos,
where the snow would still be lying above Béjar, on
through the brassy sounding provinces of Salamanca
and Zamora to the city of Leon itself, whence can be
seen the mountains of the Asturias rising like an
austere blue wall of cloud from the stony floor of the
tableland. Above Zamora the red main road forked
to the north and the west; instead of marching on
Leon I could, if I desired, turn westward by Puebla
de Sanabria into Galicia, which would be rich and
green with mountainous spring water pouring from
the mountain bodies, and emerald rivers chanting in
valleys of poplars and the vine. So, over the Sierra
of the Cat's Tail, which are piled above the northern
Portuguese frontier by Verin and by Orense, to Vigo
by Redondela. At Vigo—suitcase and return.

There was a pleasure in wielding those names in
the mind, but I thought as I was taking the Via Plata
of the Romans—that great highway which cut Spain
in two from Cadiz to Santander—I would follow
their heroic venture into Leon, at least, and eschew
that too romantic Galicia. No; I would keep to that
harder central plateau, and I would know the mono-
tony of that burned-up country, the dumbness of its
cottages and taverns. It would be unpleasant for my
body, but for the soul it would be ennobling.

I was still alone. The other occupant of the compartment had not yet taken his seat. He was evidently

standing in the corridor. Although I could not
actually see him, I could see his heavy shadow. At
Winchester the rails whirred beneath our wheels like
a lightning storm of javelins, but the train escaped
crying among the sweet, comforting meadows. The
delicate, round hills of the southern counties curved
by like a vast and leisurely green game of bowls.
There was no excitement in the game ; romantically
I looked forward to the nakedness, the poverty, the
savagery, the golden bombast, the masculinity, the
heroic barrenness of Spain. Spain like a helmet. I
thought of myself walking those 300 odd miles as a
man hungry, thirsty, exhausted with carrying the sun
like a golden ball on his shoulders over an earth of
fire. I felt I should have that fire in my limbs, that
earth in my body. Returning, I should declaim with
Spanish lassitude—after the blaze of fire the black,
cold ashes—those lines of the Andalusian, Antonio
Machado—

> 'He andado muchos caminos
> He abierto muchas veredas
> He navigado en cien mares
> Y he atracado en cien riberas'

through those restless verses to the last, which has in
four lines the essence of the Spanish genius—

> 'Y no conocen la prisa
> Ni aun en los días de fiesta
> Donde hay vino beben vino
> Donde no hay vino agua fresca.'

At this poetical and pleasant conclusion my meditation slowed down with the slowing of the train.

Southampton station was clapping slowly its white
platforms, scaring the marauding train away. I had
dozed and, rising to shake the drowsiness out of
myself, those dreams seemed to be running down my
thighs, my legs, and out of the toes of my boots.
Good legs, thought I, surveying them. The great
decisions of life are made by the legs. Instinct is
in the legs. The girding of the loins is the
theme of the Old Testament as the putting on of
bowels of mercies is the theme of the New. I have
never seen why atheists should have the monopoly
of the body. So, good legs, thought I. In praise
of legs ! An ode to legs ! The pillars of Hercules,
columnar, leading, muscular. My legs are armies,
my lips red bugles.

I became aware that my preenings had been watched
from the corridor, and by a face that was unmistak-
able, the face of a square, red-faced man who had
besides a red, folding neck ! His eyes were as shrewd
as two pips under a steam of eyebrow and, of course
I realised it now, there was a small Gladstone bag on
the rack above him. He came in and sat down for
the first time in the compartment. We were passing
through the docks. The high ranks of ships were
drawn up. There were the great names. He knew
them all. He said, addressing me genially :

' There's the *Aquitania* and that's the *Olympic*. She
gets to Cherbourg in four hours. We'll take eight.'

I sat up in astonishment. How did he know where
I was going, and on what boat ? Ah, those labels in
the tube. He wallowed in the smiles of his omni-
science. He chuckled.

He took possession of me and disarmed me. He became confidential, the courtesy of the victor towards the vanquished.

'Yus! My missus won't 'arf bust 'erself when she 'ears of this,' said he, breaking off like a serial story at the crucial point.

'Hears of what?'—he knew I would ask that.

'Garn,' said he, giving me a look that took my breath away. 'Slingin' me 'ook!'

He gave me another swipe with his eyes. I was semi-conscious, but I remember that he jumped out on to the platform before the train had stopped and ran across the sheds towards the boat. I never saw him again.

CHAPTER II.
GOOD FRIDAY

The liner was a black wall with a hole in its side, and people climbed up to her and down from her on gangways like the ladders the Lilliputians used upon Gulliver. There was a young officer standing at the top of the gangway. The pupils of his blue eyes were always poised under his lids as though he were regarding a bird in flight. I noticed him as I passed into the ship. He looked a true, young scorner of other races ; an obstinate scorner, too, for he had a long, receding chin. It always gave me a curious pleasure to watch this young man, during the voyage. There seemed a kind of mysticism in the rising gaze of those eyes of his. There are eyes that hold and fascinate and obtain a tribute of covert stares and surprised, second glances from the world. He was the type of steadfast youth outgrowing idealism into authority born to attract my restless, weaker kind. With admiration I leaned on the bulwarks later, supposedly looking down on our seething trough of foam, but actually impelled to wait on his every glance, expression, and word. At Cherbourg, La Coruña, Vigo, and Lisbon I went specially to the gangway to observe him, to hear him swear at the emigrants, and to watch him using his boot on them, as they clambered up with their bundles, sacks, and bright boxes on their backs.

The liner moved down Southampton Water with

the orchestra playing in the first-class lounge, and we in the second class received the music which poppled, crackled, and squealed its cloudy despisal of us by amplifier. The boat drifted down like an island forest of fantastic iron shapes possessed by the pervading, grinding shudder of the engines. It is said there is no adventure and no romance on the sea in these years, and that the great theme of a man struggling alone with Nature is gone for ever with the windjammers. Since when has man ceased to contend with the unknown, I wondered, as with some majesty we appeared upon the widening silver of Southampton Water ; and the grey, declaiming shapes of the docks, the cranes, the derricks, and the long sheds, the aslant squads of funnels of a score of liners, the slim factory chimneys like smokeless cannons rising out of the contracting sections of dock land, sank and diminished at the end of a lengthening, choppy wake of jazz. There was a pride in that poor music and we seemed to be marching out to the swing of it. I liked the swish-pump-clotter-crash of it, uncouth sounds from the uncouth thing I was on and, if there is no greatness nor adventure on the sea now, every man who heard those sounds must have seemed to himself as great a hero as Ulysses and pitted against as mysterious a destiny, the strange destiny of the outward bound. I wondered through whose lives I, like a ship, should pass during the next three days.

The scolding tugs dropped away. Bells rang. The engines stopped and the great thing ceased to tremble. I saw the pilot take a leap into his boat

and toss away in it. Out of our silence the engines
moved like mumbling lips again, and we passed
farther down that dull highway of water until, meeting the open sea by the Needles, it was churned into
green currents and eddies and lay a frayed and choppy
line of green against the frightened grey of the
Channel.

I hate the effort of making new acquaintances and
instinctively distrust the person who tries to engage
me in conversation. I set out with the intention
of getting a book out of the library, lowering
myself into the volume like a miner descending into
a mine, and there working at it until my short
voyage was over. I asked the steward when the
library was open. He was pale with a complexion,
chilliness, and wateriness that made me think constantly of cold mutton. Of course he had seen better
days. ' Let the pore fellers get a bit of sleep. They're
up at five,' was his reply, and prelude, to an account
of how he had lost all his money in a business deal
in Buenos Aires—' a place the British oughter've
took,' he said dismally, explaining the fundamental
reason for his failure. ' I carnt complain,' he continued complaining hard. ' I went into it with me
eyes open, and I got stung.' The shafts were well
aimed at my youth. Oh, cunning judge of character,
so pitiably bald ! Failure, loss, resignation : my
youth flinched at these blows. If I had been leaving
the boat at that moment I should have given him five
pounds and pressed his muttony hand.

At Cherbourg in the semi-darkness and drizzle, with
eight hundred Polish and Russian emigrants being

sucked aboard us and being shovelled into the bows, and a dreary fog bell tolling, there was a great Cunarder alongside us with tugs and launches champing, and breaking the darkness around her.

'Castle liner,' said the steward, glaring with a dyspeptic casualness out of the portholes, '*Edinburgh Castle.*'

I left the table in disgust. A man who had been going to sea for twenty years and did not know a Cunarder when he saw one! I should never be afraid of stewards again.

We left Cherbourg. I went up to the smoke-room, a small, shrilly varnished room, with fixed armchairs you could not sit back in, and writing-tables that were just too narrow, and which muttered, twittered, and rattled a minute orchestra of noises. A nervous, restless place in the shining panels of which you saw the twitching reflections of your fellow-passengers. We were in the panel-gazing stage, conversation was still but desultory. We were none of us more real to one another than shimmering, disembodied reflections.

The boat was a warm and musing body. If by day she had been like a fantastic island forest, she was now by night a live, huge, moving being. There was a sensuousness in her movement, in her twists of will, drama in the ring of her bell, mystery in the sliding of her masts over the floor of stars, and the black rushing of the sea sometimes in collision against her heavy flanks. She seemed to be alive—that was what pleased us—something like ourselves, pressing into the dark. We identified ourselves with her. That night I awoke many times and sat up wondering

where she was now, how far from land, and if she
could see lights anywhere; and I pictured to myself
the black and empty circle of water around her and
her jaw breaking the dividing foam.

I shared the cabin with an American and a Mexican.
The American was a quiet man of eggish complexion.
He wore a narrow white tie which looked in the
distance like a draper's tape. There was the nicety of
the draper about him. I spent my time avoiding him,
by feigning sleep in the morning when he was
getting up uncommonly early, and by coming down
late at night when he was abed, for his conversation
was unbearable. He went about apportioning information to every one. The Mexican followed him
about like a black and hairy dog. He was a man of
rich lash and eyebrow, and had the chiselled face of
the Indian. The American had several little black
attaché cases which he kept under his berth in a neat
row, and whenever he and the Mexican were together in the cabin, he would open one of the cases
and bring out a bundle of religious tracts and a few
illustrated, coloured books for children about the
life of Jesus.

The Mexican accepted some of these pamphlets
politely and put them under his pillow, but the
pictures of Jesus delighted him. A strange smile
sparkled in his eyes, sometimes tender, childish;
and sometimes I wondered if it were the amused
scepticism of an ancient race.

'I have lots more,' the American would say,
eagerly opening bag after bag. The Mexican looked
at him in wonder.

' It is a business, this of the child Jesus,' he said.

' It is,' said the American emphatically.

Travelling has shown me men are almost entirely preoccupied with the endeavours and anxieties of earning a living. That is the great adventure of the world. And after that, men have a little time for the discussion or indulgence of three more absorbing ideas : disease, religion, and love, in that order.

Disease was by far the favourite topic on board. It seemed disease was even more enjoyable than an illicit love-affair or a new religion. The glorious self-indulgence of describing in horrifying details all your symptoms and sufferings! There was a Spaniard sitting near me in the smoke-room, a man of almost violet complexion, who clung by his tendril-like fingers to a pillar in the room and hung there drooping like some exotic convolvulus. He would hang there for hours telling people about his disease. Every one was enchanted. All were en-thralled by his injured lungs, his abominable kidneys, his fatty heart, his martyrised appendix. Most of all they admired his stomach. The most diverting things had happened to his stomach. It had been the joy of half the doctors and surgeons of Europe, and its behaviour in Buenos Aires had been positively theatrical.

By one of those ironies of circumstance, this gentle-man was approached by my American, who had evidently marked him down for a tract. Before the American had time to grasp the Spaniard's soul, he was flaunting his vile body and glorying in it. He

uncurled himself from the pillar and, at the top of his
voice, began to dilate on his sufferings.

'It is my stomach,' he cried, gesticulating from that
part as though tearing out a handful of it. 'It is in a
terrible condition. It is frightful. It is loathsome.
No one knows, no one can know, what I suffer from
my stomach. A year ago I left Buenos Aires to con-
sult doctors in Europe. I have been cut open in
three directions. My stomach has been removed,
studied, turned upside down,' he became greatly
excited and made slowly the gruesome motion of
turning a stomach upside down. 'It has been
X-rayed, sewn up, perforated. It has been filled with
drugs as a bagpipes is with wind. I have gone without food, and it has been as empty as a squeezed and
shrivelled orange.' He squeezed his hands together
and wrung them out. 'It is the intestines. Death is
in my intestines. They have been raised. They have
been lowered. Everything that is possible to do
with one's intestines has been done to mine.' He
unbuttoned his waistcoat and his trousers. He lifted
up his shirt and vest. The Spaniards in the knot of
listeners moved forward. The English drew back.

'Do you see the scars? That was the last. The
other three are previous ones. At one time my
stomach was almost green to look at. Indeed,' cried
he in triumph, 'the doctor in Berlin said my intestines were fantastic, that never in his life had he seen
such fantastic intestines as mine.'

The Spaniard lowered his shirt and vest. He but-
toned up his trousers and waistcoat. He paused and
looked around for the murmur of sympathy that

promptly came. He shrugged his shoulders, ' There
you are ! So we are made, poor creatures ! '

He was the hero of the evening. He curled himself
once more round the pillar. There was a genial old
doctor, rotund and with a Punch-like nose, and a head
as bald as a ripe melon. His goodness was spoiled
by a marauding desire to discover a ' fourth ' for
bridge. There were three bridge players : the
doctor. The ' buck '—as I called him—who might
have come straight out of ' Polly,' for he had the leg
and the figure, and moreover a way of wagging his
finger at you as though you were a pretty chamber-
maid. His face was as fresh as salmon. And the
missionary, a youngish, blue-eyed man, with a
modest, ginger moustache, which the doctor declared always put him in mind of primitive Christianity, ' growing surreptitiously and daily persecuted by the sword.'

The three players were in the smoke-room when
the story of the fantastic stomach had been told ;
indeed they had perforce stopped their game to
listen, for the Spaniard had filled the air like a hurdy-
gurdy. The missionary, being young enough to
want to make himself heard by riper men, said the
story reminded him of a vicious kind of tick to be
found in East Africa. The ' buck ' talked about the
blood-sucking parasites his brother had told him
about in Mauritius. The doctor waited for his
moment and capped all with a nauseating story
about a Chinaman who had had a boil which behaved
like a volcano. The doctor told the story slowly,
precisely, in professional language, which gave it a

special cruelty and made the 'buck' and the missionary involuntarily rub the backs of their necks.

The 'buck,' pale as so pink a man could become, turned the conversation abruptly to the topic that invariably follows that of disease. He said—'I saw in a bookshop the other day a book called "The Philosophy of Religion"'—with a slightly nervous drawl he affected as a man of parts, and looking hopefully at the missionary. The missionary smiled gratefully and wetted his lips to begin, but the doctor was too quick for him.

'Cut,' said he deeply. And they went on playing.

I agreed with the doctor. I spend my life avoiding other people's religions. That evening I went down late to the cabin particularly to avoid the American's religion. I dreaded he would open those little black bags neatly rowed under his berth like shoes, for me. As I went down it seemed the long, swaying vista of white corridor was a catacomb with numbered sepulchres; on either side the entrances to the enamel tombs. They were quiet and warm: a steward rippled noiselessly round a corner like a straying spirit. There was a gentle motion in the bay, and the air was thick, woven with a myriad, nervous motions. The Mexican, whose dark hair shone like some rich exotic fern on his pillow, had fallen asleep with one of the missionary's picture-books open in his hand.

On the morning after the second night we arrived at La Coruña. It was seven o'clock. The sea was running high and royally blue under a windy lace of

spume in a great rush southward. Body after body
of blue water was borne up loftily and broke into
an ecstasy of foam, slid into dark and luminous
troughs. There was a solidity and yet a lightness in
the water. Each wave was a being. It rose, flew,
arched downwards with the deliberation of a school
of porpoises, and the sun drenched the south-eastern
middle distance with a blending, heavy area of silver.
The fishing-boats under their sling of sail flew into
La Coruña ahead of us, like gulls. The foam spat
up on them in radiant showers, the water splintered
on them like glass. Now they lay flat as a web of
surf on one wave, now they were leaping or diving
for the next one. They slit wind and sea with their
speed, and spume could not fly faster or sting harder.
Beyond them the mountainous coast lumped hotly
down in heavy ore-like masses under a sky of
infinite, diamond azure as clear as wind, and as we
steamed into the Bay and as its headlands reached
out round us, I saw white Coruña rooted along the
sea's edge-like teeth on the jawbone of Sierra that
lay behind it.

The launches cut across to meet us, plumed with
foam. The missionary had been up on deck an hour
taking his exercise and snapping a sharp good
morning to every one. The American and the
Mexican were prowling about like two dogs, pawing
each other, looking at each other, smiling and not
talking much. After a while the ' buck ' came up
and soon put us in a state of excitement. He walked
from deck to deck eagerly crying, ' Where is it ?
Have you all seen it ? '

' Seen what ? ' we asked.

' The monument ! The monument, of course. The monument to Sir John Moore.'

' But who was Sir John Moore ? ' asked the American, preparing solemnly to acquire information.

' Good heavens, sir,' cried the ' buck ' flushing, and drawing himself up with a click of the heels.

> ' Not a drum was heard, not a funeral note,
> As his corpse to the rampart we hurried,
> Not a soldier discharged his farewell shot
> O'er the grave where our hero we buried.
> We buried him darkly at dead of night,
> The sods with our bayonets turning . . .'

he declaimed, flinging grand gestures from his bosom until every one but the American left him ; there was what is called an honest tear in his worthy face.

The doctor led me away by the arm to the starboard side, and whispered confidentially, ' Did you ever have to parse that ? '

There was a rowing-boat bobbing up and down at the foot of our high, black wall. There were no other craft on this side, and from the boat the crane was hauling up an enormous quarter of beef, as if surreptitiously, hurriedly, for fear any of the passengers should see it.

' Saw a nigger crushed by a bale of stuff like that in Mogador, twenty years ago,' said the doctor in dry, reminiscent tone and on the favourite theme again. ' Broken spine. They brought him up to me. I couldn't do anything with him. He didn't make a sound, but lay staring at me dumbfounded until they took him ashore.'

There was great confusion on the second-class
deck and in the water below, cries, blasphemy, the
human struggle. I went round as usual to watch my
young officer. He stood scornfully at the top of the
gangway, up which climbed the frightened emigrants
—short, hot men in blue boinas, from the hot, spring
mountains of Galicia and the Asturias. They carried
their sacks and precious bright boxes on their
shoulders. There was one man carrying his long saw,
with a strip of cane to protect its teeth, to cut down
the trees of the New World. How many had that
saw cut down in the Old ? Up the high wall of the
ship they climbed those shouting, goaded creatures.
They smelled of beasts and of the earth, and their
faces were rough and red as the soil. They struggled
up like an indefatigable column of ants irritating the
ship. The young officer, eyes lifted to a heaven of his
own, cursed them. There were two old men clam-
bering and shouting their way up hoarsely, almost
on all fours with a heavy tin trunk. They grappled
with it, clutched it, strained at it, as though it were a
thing as dear as life. The sweat poured from them ;
now one was underneath, now the other. At one
moment it was about to fall on them and fling them
back into the sea, but the next moment they were
conquering, holding it down. It kicked like a beast.
The two old men screeched and fought the thing
like monkeys.

' Get on ! Haven't you any guts, you dam dagos ? '
shouted my young man, and gave them a push with
his boot as at last they crawled past him too excited
and anxious to be aware of anything but their box,

which for those anxious minutes had been like a
world toppling against their bodies.

A native doctor grabbed the two men — as he
grabbed all the emigrants, men and children—and
put a match under their eyelids and seemed to turn
their eyes inside out in ghastly fashion, stared into
their mouths, and gave them a smack on the back
before they knew where they were.

Disputes with boatmen, money changers, and post-
card sellers soon sprang up among the peasants. In
a moment the deck was in an uproar. The only quiet
man was the carabinero, who leaned against the bulwarks with his gun between his knees, gazing at the
crowds with the completest disdain, as though glad
the boat was going to take the pestilential creatures
away. Now and then he turned round and spat with
official dignity into the sea.

On the chief public buildings of the town—the bar-
racks, the various forts on the hill around, the Town
Hall, and the Customs House—the red and yellow
Spanish flag was flying, but beyond this there was
nothing to indicate Spain. I could see a green avenue
by the harbour wall, and up and down the avenue
ones and twos of little black specks were moving.
People. Who were they, and what were they saying?
The barren, boulder-strewn hills receded along the
coast like mailed arms thrown back into the blue bays
of the southern distance and raised on either side of the
town like the arms of a crucifix. For a few minutes a
bare hill of sand came to life as a troop of miniature
cavalry petered out of the fort on top of it and can-
tered down the hill on to a road where they raised a

cottony cloud of dust. They were riding towards
the town.

The American, in an attempt to buttonhole the
' buck,' had been buttonholed by him instead. The
' buck,' flushed by his recital of the ' Burial of Sir
John Moore,' and explaining with some rhetoric that
the British were never so glorious as when they were
defeated, drifted to the story of his own life, and told
how he was the Conservative whip for Blankshire,
where his party had been gloriously and splendidly
defeated for the last thirty-five years. He added, at a
tangent, that what the working-classes needed was
more religion to keep them in their places.

' If they haven't a good, sound religion of some
kind or other to give them ballast,' he said, ' they
get carried away by some clever fellow.'

I heard that as I leaned gazing over the harbour to the
early town. It was at this moment that I noticed the
hot Spanish flag was flying at half-mast. I wondered
what great personage had died. Perhaps a prime
minister, an archbishop, a public man of sorts, even
one of Spain's eight hundred generals. It was clearly
an occasion of official mourning, and no people love
death as the Spaniards love it. They enjoy the evidence of death. They love the sight of a good, bloody
corpse, well gashed and bruised—who can forget the
revolting realism of the agonised Christs of their
galleries and processions ?—the years of mourning,
the months of lament, the lugubrious pomp of their
funerals, in short, the deification of the word that is
oftenest on their lips, ' Nada '—nothing, vacuum.

I was bold enough to ask the carabinero. I said, ' I

see the flag is at half-mast in the town. Who has died in Spain ? '

He turned on me, and his eyes were musingly half-closed like a cat's. There was a darkness like the bloom of grapes in them, and whether the glitter was of infinite sadness or the token of an ancient irony I could not tell. He said, ' It is our Lord Jesus Christ, the Son of God.'

I remembered then that it was Good Friday.

CHAPTER III

THE DARK WOMAN RUNNING

When I heard those words of the carabinero I knew at last I had touched Spain. We steamed out of La Coruña in a deepening blue heat, hot Spain lying to the east of us, its torrid, brown and sapphire slabs of land beyond a raw sea. The wide boat of black iron pushed forward and trod down the waves, and we were borne moodily in a dream of blue. In time the wind dropped and we began to feel the sun. He seemed to circle rampaging up the sky. His light was in my bones, my eyes, my hair. My whole body was drinking the sunlight and it enriched me. At the sight and the touch of its gold my spirit opened as the hand for money, and the mind sank, as it were, *into* the body until I was nothing but senses, warm, indolent, and happy. The sunlight burned the cheeks and blurred the sight with a pleasant ache of drowsiness, penetrating and enveloping my deep being. Hours slid by one into another like murmurs from the sleeping lips of time. I lay on deck as one carried voluptuously southward on blue wings. In the afternoon the sun became barbarous and sent down his light to beat a strident glitter of music in the sea, the incessant beating of a million blinding machines.

At Vigo there was the usual scene. We appeared out of our blue world of flame in that majestic bay, as the escorting mountains opened out range after range, peak after peak, withdrawing like the per-

sonages of a gigantic court. The tugs and launches
aimed slowly out to meet us, dazed arrows released
from a white pyramid town of sleep.

The ship's purser, a sardonic youth, collected his
documents and stood at the door of his glum little
office in the stern, waiting for the sundry officials, the
strange miscellany who came aboard at every port.

'Ah! Here they come, covered in diamonds like
young chorus girls,' cried he, as the officials came up
the corridor.

'Hail, King of Vigo!' he mocked gravely, as a stout
and fantastically dressed gentleman headed the party.
'And shaved, too. The King has shaved!'

The 'King' was delighted. He was a short and
corpulent man with the girth of a barrel. He had
three separate globes of chin pending below an ever
open mouth, from which his breath bubbled as he
walked along. He was like an enormous codfish.
His grey eyebrows were curled like fins. His grey
hair, in which there was a yellow stain, as though he
had once tried to dye it, was waved, and he wore on a
monumental nose a pair of pince-nez with a black
ribbon to them. His clothes surpassed even the
elaboration of his figure. Under a tight grey coat of
incredible waist he wore a pale blue embroidered
waistcoat with a white piqué lining. Under his wing
collar was bunched a large black and white silk stock
with a diamond pin in it. His trousers were Oxford,
biscuit colour, and he wore coffee-coloured spats
over yellow suede shoes. His little fat fingers were
phosphorescent with rings, and he had a pink carna-
tion in his buttonhole.

The purser admired his spats. 'Café au lait,' the purser said, indicating the subtle colour.

The 'King' inflated himself to his full corpulence like a speckled frog. He was delighted. He pulled up his trousers to reveal an atrocious pair of red, yellow, and green ringed silk socks !

'Compote de fruits,' laughed the 'King' readily. 'Zee Savile Row !' and sat down with great difficulty at the purser's desk to blow on a nest of documents. At any moment I expected to see air-bubbles rise from his lips or his ears as he sat, nay, almost lay there, shaking like a fish.

The sun dropped down behind the westward mountains of Vigo Bay and the mighty ranges simplified and darkened into one jagged violet line of Sierra : a saw, above the teeth of which the sky was ice green and whitened with the glow of the west. A delicate jewelry of lights appeared on the long miles of the bay's edge, and lights ticked out and moved on the three huge island promontories of the Cies, forms that sealed the bay and beyond which were the dark and the open sea.

Noiseless dusk came down like a sweet veiling incense over the sea, a wide and gentle, dark bosom, as we steamed out. The lights of Vigo, that little white pyramid, sent chains and lances of gold plunging into the water, which gathered together and glittered like a constellation of rare,·earth-fallen stars as the night grew luxurious in darkness, and were slowly effaced by an indigo stratum of headland moving irresistibly out into the ocean.

The lights of villages were raked together like

star dust on the black mountain shapes, and at times
I would be watching with minute excitement for the
growing and lessening of a lighthouse's blobbed
beam. Above us was a full, hot white star pushed up
the sky and sliding down it again over Portugal, as
the ship rolled, and I could hear below the soft
swirling of the combed water and could see the wav-
ing line of jagged Portugal streaming past as though
it were the long hair of a dark woman running
southward with us through the night. The night
was warm and the breath of land was strong with
wild odours of lavender, thyme, sage, and the oak
scrub of the bearded Portuguese mountains, and as I
lay watching the up beat of that white star I wished
the ship might go out and out for ever and be heard
of no more, that we might dissolve at the supreme
moment of the ecstasy like the breaking of a rising
wave. The Keatsian mood,

> ' To cease upon the midnight with no pain.'

We lacked only a nightingale, but soon a barbarous
Eastern music flared sporadically from the steerage
deck. The Spanish emigrants, who during their first
few hours aboard had been desolate, were now
beginning to feel more cheerful. They flung themselves on the decks, making pillows of their sacks.
The men lay flat on their backs with cigars in their
mouths. The women, shawled and with bright
yellow scarves hooded about their necks, and earrings
darting back and forth like tiny, gilt, coiled serpents
from their ears, sat upright, staring at the passing
darkness—goddesses awaiting the fulfilment of a

prophecy. The men began to sing, and at last the
voice of a man lying full length on the deck, with
his head propped up on a woman's lap and a cigar
dulling and brightening in his mouth, singled itself
out. A harsh, crying voice in that twanging African
minor, as though the words were being wrenched
out of the mouth of a body contracting with barbarous agony, which sang these words—

> ' Somos pobres muchachos de Cadiz-z-z-z
> No sabemos apuntar-ar-ar,
> A las muchachas de Cadiz-z-z-z
> Se las puede preguntar-ar-ar.'

There was another verse to that which I did not
catch. After each song there would be lively talk,
badgering, and jeering, and then, after a raucous spit
and a puff at the cigar, again the man's voice would
assert itself like a desert cry, but with that Spanish
irony, the bitterness of which is buried in resignation—

> ' Mi padre manda a mi madre-e-e-e-e
> Y mi madre me manda a mi-i-i-i
> Y mi madre me manda a mi-i-i
> *(quickly)*
> Yo mando a mis hermanos
> Todos nos mandamos aqui-i-i-i-i-i.'

The ironic emphasis of derision of the last line shot
out like anarchy triumphant. Again, two lines from
a fisherman's song, beautiful, but a sardonic hint of
death in that beauty as there is in all the dark,
beautiful things of Spain—

> ' Digame pesca a brillante
> Donde estan sus niños.'

And another brave one in challenging tones, the
song of the men of Pravia in the Asturias, whence all
the able-bodied young men go to South America—

> ' Soy de Pravia-a-a,
>   Y mi madre una praviana-a-a-a ;
>   Y por eso en mi no cabe
>   Partida ninguna mala.'

(I am from Pravia, and my mother a Praviana ; for
this reason there is no evil in me.)

As the hours passed by this man lay there breaking
into sporadic song. Four men began to dance with a
great deal of heel stamping and snapping of fingers.
The Arab was in that stamping and that rhythm. It
seemed to rise in a vibrant, almost visible wall about
them, to rouse the senses by its thousand agitations,
its checked, spiralling notes of passion, humour, and
aged custom. The dust rose from the deck, there
was a vapour of crackling feet ; bodies, arms, and
heads swaying and wagging loosely like marionettes
on a string, till, as the effort became fiercer and more
strained, the women got up and began beating their
hands in time and shouting, ' Anda ! Anda ! Anda ! '
harshly as though they were crying to beasts they
were driving. Up and down, the white star slid
about the mast as the boat swayed to the ancient
motions of the sea.

In the morning I landed at Lisbon. I left the
American, who was typing in the lounge much to
every one's annoyance. The ' buck ' was going
ashore. The doctor was greeted by a Portuguese
friend, who presented him with an embarrassing

bouquet of red and white roses, behind which he seemed more faun-like, more Punch-like than ever, a crowned Bacchus. The blue-eyed missionary stamped energetically up and down the deck in tennis flannels, with a neat little theological step and giving a nervous touch to primitive Christianity now and then. He glanced sometimes at the hot sight of Lisbon, with its houses like white, red-lidded boxes heaped on a score of hills, as though he would think about all that later.

'I wonder if there will be a revolution,' said the 'buck,' as he prepared to go down to the launch.

CHAPTER IV.
NOTHING ABOUT PORTUGAL

I know nothing about Portugal except that its railway system must be the worst in the world, and that at the great Roccio Station in Lisbon the only visible word—and it is placarded in enormous fiery letters across the booking hall—is one we seem to have heard of before: Keatings.

CHAPTER V.
BEFORE BADAJOZ

I arrived from Lisbon at the station of Badajoz between five and six in the morning. The station—as often happens in Spain—lay nearly two miles from the town. I turned my back on the green slopes of Portugal. There was no one in the station except a bent, wrinkled old porter who nearly wept when I told him I was not going to Seville, but whether because of the compliment to Badajoz or the slight to Seville I could not see. I set out down the long hill from the station, my pack on my back, and with him giving the pack its baptism of Spanish stare. No one can stare as the Spaniard does. It is not a nervous, askance gaze, but a man-to-man, full-faced, and rather lordly stare, fixed, large-eyed, and oriental as though the starer had gone into a trance. The Spaniard stares with his whole body. I felt that porter penetrating me, permeating me, possessing me like a Dybbuk, as I walked down the avenue.

I walked those two miles with trembling limbs. I see already I am exaggerating : the distance was two kilometres, but on an empty stomach it might have been a league. Tremble of excitement at seeing pale Spain stretched out before dawn and awaiting my feet ; tremble of sunless chill. The stars had died out of that high dome of Spanish night, and the sky of immense blue arched over the sap-green plains of

Extremadura to a lilac breath of Sierra, on an horizon
twenty or thirty miles away. The east fluttered like a
bird, but there was not a cloud to catch its gold. I
saw before me a wide country, green with young
crops and rippling like a lake of small hills and still
pasturage. There were faint sweeps of pink land and,
but for the marching acacias on the road, no trees.
There was the tall April barley near-by, and as I
walked down, mists white as daisies were appearing in the lower fields where long men were
cutting the barley for forage, and singing to themselves.

In the vast pink and green plain before me I could
see no villages. There were one or two white farms,
riding like sea birds on the hill crests, and although
they seemed within hand grasp, I knew in the pointed
clarity of the Spanish air they must be leagues away.
To stand breathing such pale draughts of distance
before sunrise liberated the spirit as though I had
breathed infinity—

> ' For he on honey-dew hath fed
> And drunk the milk of Paradise.'

—and to awaken that desire to wander endlessly
from place to place, which is the essence of the
Spanish genius. I was impatient to attain that faint
movement of Sierra I had seen to the north, and by
which I conjectured my route would lie, desiring to
be there as one might desire a star ; but inwardly
fearful of the labour of getting there. Shaking the
fear out of my head by another step into the imagination : in a week, I thought, I shall have outstepped

even this infinite. As I walked down the broad
avenue the sweetness of the acacias was in the air, the
smell of fresh meadows too, and of that strong
lavender which is like incense. Spain was as sweet
as young grass, and those odours and that air rose
thrilling in the limbs like a sap.

From every field sprang the early songs of the
solitary workers. Along the road—its soft, floury
dust still warm with the noon of the day before—
padded donkeys to the fields or the towns. The
riders were tall, big-boned men, with steep-crowned
hats on their heads, and as they jogged along, their
legs kicked up and down, their bodies shook list-
lessly, and there was not a smile on their long, tanned
faces. They sang musingly to themselves as they
travelled till every road, path, and field had a song
in it. Slow minor melodies :

> ‘ Mi madre dice a mi novia-a-a-a
>   Que soy capaz . . .’

broken off into a surprised humming, as staring they
passed me, and the stare broken by a sudden cry to
the donkey,
> ‘ Burra-a-a-a ! ! ! ’

stirring a warm foam of dust. A road of acacias and
songs.

The road sank to the river, the Guadiana, that
bright water more precious than jewels to this
country. The river combed down in silver over a
broad dam, sweeping round in full view of the city,
binding it on two sides, and passing under a massive

bridge of twenty-eight arches. The river bed was a wide stretch of shingle which would glare like antimony when the sun got up ; only under the central arches poured a narrow throat of water, half-way on its journey from the broken heights of the Sierra Morena to the sea. The enormous bridge trod across that wide bed clumsily, high and dry, unnecessarily huge like some prehistoric creature. But, in the winter, I was told the bridge was sunken in flood water as red as blood, and the gypsies who had built themselves shacks of beaten tins and branches would have to flee for their lives, often losing all their property, but always coming back to the same places again when the waters had gone down.

The town was heaped beyond the bridge, a low broad mound of heavy red roofs, one above the other like a pile of earthenware dish-covers, with only a white slit of wall showing here and there, and not a window or a chimney visible. An Arab town for the Arab songs. A city as flat as a stork's nest, and crowned by a church spire which itself might have been a stork. Round the city was a belt of yellow walls. To the north were the ruins of an old Moorish tower, a bulky thing like a cabin trunk standing on end, and, but for the tower, a stranger might never have noticed the city as he passed, with its roofs crammed down over its ears and its walls half-hidden by the barley.

As I crossed the narrow bridge, the donkeys and mules increased and the songs with them. A gypsy was singing in his shack by the river. He was making fish snares out of rushes. I could see at the end of the bridge the obese city gates, with officials and peasants scattered brightly like confetti about them. The sun leapt flying out of the plain like a lark rising in a song of light, and with that light the distances hardened and darkened, the green of the pastures became vivid and shrill, and the soil as red as infantry. The breath of Sierra became a flame, and before it there appeared dramatically a dark line of wilderness which the flame seemed to be consuming.

The officials blinked at me as I passed under the gate. I muttered a nervous ' Buenos Dias ! ' and I was nearly out of earshot before an equally jerky ' Vaya . . . ' came from them. A cold reception, a surprised reception. I should have remembered to bawl my greetings genially from at least fifteen yards' range. A shy whisper is a thing no Spaniard understands. If he stares, his body stares. If he speaks, his body speaks. I walked into the town deciding to shout at the next man.

The streets were narrow, tortuous, tangled like string, and cobbled. The houses were two stories high, with iron balconies and barred windows as though each house were a prison, shutting out the sun. The sun had not yet a firm hold on the sky. Few people were astir. Sometimes from a doorway there clawed a sickly stench of charcoal burning. Stealthy, clammy smells of stale vinegar, olive oil, and wine put their hands out of courtyards as I passed. Each street was named in big, black, childish letters. There were flowers in some of the balconies. The town tram, a weird vehicle like a yellow milk cart, drawn by three mules, bumped down the street. It had just occurred to the driver he might meet the train.

By one street and another I came at last upon the fonda, the door of which was wide open although the place was in darkness. I walked up and down tiled dirty corridors from one smell to another, making as much noise as possible. No one came. Then I found an old man in corduroy asleep on a mattress under the stairs. I shouted at him. He got up with what dignity he could collect, rubbed his face with a handkerchief, put on a hat with a pink band to it, and went grumbling and expectorating about the place, slamming open shutters, kicking at doors. Then he came back and read a newspaper. I hurled a reminder of my existence at him. ' Patience ! Patience ! ' he cried. ' Soon, soon—I suppose you— came by the train and —— ' He was asleep.

I tapped on his shoulder and asked him again, ' What about a room and some breakfast ? '

' Fill up the form,' said he.

I filled up the form with a pen that scratched like rending calico.

He was asleep again.

After half an hour a woman unloaded a big iron stove from a donkey, and installing the stove outside the fonda door, lit a charcoal fire and began to fry churros. Passers-by stopped to watch or to eat what were virtually long strips of doughnut fried in oil. The reek of such pleasant frying woke up the little man who went out and bought a yard or two of churros for my breakfast. They were cut into little coils like brown serpents, and were hung on a thread of straw.

'Patience! Patience!' said he again, seeing me pace up and down. After that I seem to have sat down in the passage and to have fallen asleep myself.

CHAPTER VI

THE EGOTIST OF BADAJOZ

I drank a grubby bowl of lukewarm coffee and ate my churros in the dining-room of the fonda, a smelly, stale sort of room with sandy-yellow plush curtains weighted with dust, and with a bar at one end of it. Here two men were quarrelling loudly about the Holy Week processions. They were both dark, oily-haired young men, and were highly excited. One declared the other's committee was bringing disgrace to the city by the disreputable appearance of one of the Virgins that had been carried round on Good Friday. But the offender was obdurate, and kept crying repeatedly, ' Nothing—but nothing ! ' And when he found that did not stop his friend, he shot up his arms with an angry cry and shouted, ' Nothing—nothing—nothing, man ! ! ' and raged out of the fonda.

I found the entrance to my room barred by ladders, pails, and boards ; while I had been breakfasting, an attack of whitewashing had sprung up. The place was in confusion. I went out and spent the day exploring the city, to attune—if that is the word—my nostrils to the smells of the country and my stomach to the food.

Each country has its smell : Spain reeks of rank olive oil. The fumes of that oil, which is used by the peasants for lighting their fires, for burning in their lamps, and for cooking their food, hit out from every doorway with a blow that at first sickened. I struggled for two days with the stink, and then it conquered me, sank into me, and permeated my system, gripped my limbs, possessed my palate, pervaded my nose—in fact, behaved like a Spanish stare so that henceforth I noticed it no more—and ate it unknowingly—the abominable stuff.

In that first day I attacked Badajoz from all angles, penetrated it by all streets, rather too consciously in search of adventure. I supposed it to be a city of twenty or thirty thousand inhabitants, and, as the city gates announced in childish black letters, ' Capital of the province of that name.' There were the usual churches and convents, full stomached and ochreous, with small barred windows set high out of reach, like dungeon gratings. There was a sun-spaced Plaza with acacias sweetly patterned in it, and from behind them the yellow mass of the Cathedral rising, a hot, stout, and pompous little place, like a country priest who had been doing himself too well. Its door was old, cunning, burned up, and drowsy as a peasant's face. I sat for an hour in the café opposite deafened by the clatter of conversation, regarding that church—I enjoyed the way the sun burned its sandstone, till it was as ripe as a golden Stilton. It ate too much that church—too many tithes, too many souls, too many priests, too much sun. It slept too much. Its bell snored harshly the hours.

The streets of Badajoz were as white as those of Seville, and they were roofed by the purple heat. They were white gulfs of heat down which women poured, carrying water-jars on their heads, and men

piped their goats through and sold the milk. There
was a man with scales on his back selling the tasteless white cheese of Extremadura. I flattened myself
against a wall or slipped out of the heat into a cold
doorway, to let pass a procession of donkeys carrying cans of milk, or baskets of oranges like red-hot
coals, or a struggling sack of chickens tied together
in bunches by the legs. Half-naked children were
leading the Easter lambs, poor be-ribboned creatures
looking as wooden and frightened as the toys of a
Noah's Ark. In the courtyards, where all was flowers
and sunlight, women were sewing, or nursing their
babies.

The cries of the streets were unforgettable. The air
was split and bludgeoned by them. The cries of the
mothers to their children—

'Maria!!! Ven aca-a-a-a!!'
'Luisa-a-a-a!!! Andate!!'—

might have split a rampart. Church bells and black-
smith's anvils could not outring the voices of the
women of Badajoz. The iron of those vowels!

Badajoz was as oriental as Tunis. It was little more
than an Arab Kasbah. The heat was glutinous in
those vehement little streets and alleys, where the
flies dazed the heat, where every crack and every
incision in the walls was pierced by the glare, and
you could see a fly thirty yards away. Every doorstep
had its trade. There were carpenters, smiths, wheel-
wrights, cart makers, basket makers, and innumerable
little booths and shops. You could buy lizards,
snails, and frogs in one street. The activity and the
agitation were constant. But of all places in the

town the market-place was the most agitated. It was
at the northern end of the town in an aged, whitewashed Moorish Plaza under the tower of the old
fort. In the Plaza stood the public weighbridge, the
market stalls, and the Parador del Sol, a cavernous
inn sunken under low and profound archways, and
more like an enormous wine vault than anything else.
Here peasants arrived on their donkeys and mules,
and stabled them there among the provisions and
the huge barrels, while the innkeeper's wife cooked a
lively dish of cocido—pork, beans, garlic, pimento,
and oil—on a little heap of charcoal on the pavement
outside, and kept an eye on three or four babies as
well. After lunch I pushed my way through the sky
to the Moorish Plaza again. I have never felt such
heat. It grasped one like a fire. One made even for
an inch of shade under a high wall, but the white
walls themselves were like ovens. The heat seemed
thick, dense, and a power. When I got to the Plaza
it was deserted. I might have been the only person
in the city at that hour.

I waited under the aqueous curves of the cool
arcade of the Plaza, where there was no one but a
young man stretched on the pavement half-asleep,
when I heard the sharp sound of a jar seller. He
passed round the Plaza driving his jar-laden donkey
clinking before him.

' Botijero-o-o-o,' he cried, plunging his voice into
that tank of sun. He pushed his high-crowned hat
on the back of his head. The sweat veined his face.

' Quien quiere botija-a-a-as ? ' he cried again.
His face was long, tanned, and horse-like. He wore

corduroys and white canvas slippers. He carried a
yellow stick with a pattern stamped the length of it.
He listened. There was no reply but a crackling
volley from the storks above. He drove his donkey
under the archway down towards the river.

' Where are you going ? ' I called.

He stopped and stared at me.

' Across the province to Caceres, northwards,' he
said simply. He drew himself up proudly and
spanked the little black donkey, and watched me
again. ' He has crossed the Pyrenees once.' And
away he went crying his round, brown water-
jars.

As I walked down the street by which the jar seller
had ascended, I passed a weighty stone cellar half
above ground. It was piled up with sacks of flour,
beans, grain, potatoes, and from the ceiling hung
long poles of brown sausages coiled like grubs
around them, and white strips of bacalao or cod
pending like the bodies of sinister moths. Sitting
on a sack in the doorway was an old man propped
up and cushioned by a comfortable round of stomach.
He had spectacles on the end of his nose, and he was
reading a large, black book.

It is a startling thing to find any one reading in a
Spanish town, but when that town is Badajoz and
the man a shopkeeper—and not a young man either
—the sight is as amazing as a prophecy. I asked the
man what he was reading. He replied enigmatically :

' It is a book more people ought to read.'

He continued to read. I said it must be a very
interesting book.

'It is,' he said.

I asked what it was about.

'It tells you everything you want to know,' he said, his eyes looking up and full of tantalising amusement.

'An encyclopædia?' I said.

'Much more,' said he.

'Who is the author?' I cried.

'God,' said the old man.

'But —— ' I exclaimed.

'It is the Book of Genesis,' said he.

'The Book of Genesis,' I cried in amazement; 'I did not know it was possible to buy the Bible in Badajoz. I thought it was forbidden.'

Though I spend my time dodging those two great preoccupations of men, religion and disease, they jump at me from every corner. I little knew into what an ambuscade I had fallen this time.

I was seized suddenly from behind by the shoulder and pushed aside with violence. I saw the young man who before had been lying half-asleep under the arcade in the Plaza, standing between me and the old man.

His eyes were alive with a thousand little flashing black suns of excitement. His lips were trembling in his yellow oval face. He cried, 'Who are you, saying the Bible cannot be bought in Badajoz? It is a lie! It is a lie, I tell you! The Bible can be bought easily, and no one can stop it. Not even the Church of Rome which spreads all these lies about the books and tells us it is blasphemous, heretical, anti-Spanish. We know their methods here. They create an air of mystery about it because they hate and fear the truth ! They dread the day when the poor will shake off the power of the priests and think for themselves.'

The words buffeted me like fists. I could not turn away, one way or the other. I was hemmed in by his words and his gestures. I remembered catching a confused glimpse of a gypsy sitting on the curb near-by peeling an orange and throwing the vivid peel into the glare.

' This ignorance and this hate is the curse of Spain, the curse of the world ! ' went on the little man. ' You do not realise that all the calamities of the world are concentrated in this city, from the supreme crimes of ambition, egotism, and materialism downwards, and how many know the only salvation, the only key to the real life which is spiritual, lies in this book ? '

He gripped me by the shoulders, ' Here life is corrupt from top to bottom, man is evil and horrible. There is no honour, no hope, no truth in this materialism. A man becomes inspired, but egotism and ambition beset him, and his inspiration becomes a means to worldly advancement. Religion : it has become a business deal. No, we must live for one another, for the salvation of the world, for humanity. . . .'

He whirled on as self-contained as a little solar system, impervious to any of the remarks, protests, exclamations which I commenced from time to time. He clutched his hands to his bosom as though dragging a soul out of himself, speaking, as the

Spanish do speak, with his whole body. And continuing :

' What is the father's love for his child but egotism, the instinct of possession in regard to what he has created. Ah, my dear man, you must realise you are the custodian not the possessor of things. . . .'

At that moment there called the loud bosomed voice of a dark young woman from the corner of the Plaza, ' Don Benito, I want some buttons.'

He turned from me with concern and ran to the corner, where I saw he had a booth of silks, laces, mirrors, and combs and trinkets. He was clearly a haberdasher.

' Silver buttons or black ? ' he asked, but she was in no hurry to decide that. At last he came hurrying back across the cobbled sunlight to me, pocketing a ha'penny. He had lost the strand of his discourse.

' What was I saying ? ' he asked. ' Ah, yes, humanity, wasn't it ? Yes, we must live for humanity.'

' I sce you are a socialist,' I said for the tenth time, and this time the remark penetrated that thick atmosphere of incomprehension, of mental deafness which surrounds all Spaniards.

' I am not,' he said quickly. ' The socialist is a materialist and an egotist. In the end everything is corrupted by egotism ; that which was an ideal becomes a job.'

' You have travelled widely,' I suggested.

' I am from the city of Caceres. I lived there up to ten years ago, so it cannot be said that I have travelled. I was not even in Morocco. I drew a lucky number.'

'You and I are different,' I said, hurriedly getting a
word in before the next outburst. 'I believe in
travelling. I have travelled here from London to
Badajoz. I am not only going to Caceres, where you
say you were born, but I am going to continue
northward to Leon, perhaps to Vigo itself.' His
silence made me boastful. I repeated :

'Across Extremadura, northward to Plasencia,
Béjar, and into Salamanca and Zamora.' I rolled
the high sounding names on my tongue. 'On foot ! '

Don Benito went as yellow as a lemon and his jaw
dropped. He stepped back into the street incredu-
lously staring at me. A woman was coming down
the street on her donkey, with two pigs squeezing
their squealing faces out of the panniers. I pulled
the speechless Don Benito into safety. At last he
spoke.

'Walking,' he said slowly, as though trying the
amazed syllables on his palate. 'But . . . walking,
man ? On foot ? To Caceres, to Béjar, to . . . to . . .
Salamanca ? It . . . is . . . not possible, on foot ! ! '

'Yes, yes ! ' I said triumphantly and with immense
calm, enjoying his bewilderment.

Then he turned on me as quick as a whip, 'Why ? '
he snapped out.

Now that was what I myself had not decided. The
purposelessness of the journey was a constant worry
to my conscience. Don Benito had asked the question which every one would ask. 'Why ? ' Remembering my line of march would be by the great
Roman road, the Via Plata, and that by this line also
Wellington advanced in the Peninsular War, I

tossed up, as it were, the Roman road and the Duke
in my mind, and decided for the Duke.

'I am following the advance of the Duke of Wellington in the Peninsular War,' I said.

I am convinced Don Benito had never heard
of the Peninsular War, and that, even supposing
he had heard of it, he, like all other Spaniards,
would have had no idea that the English were concerned in it, such is the traditional ingratitude of
allies. As a moralist, he was right. For what concern
have the moralists with history ? He flung out his
arms in derision.

'Man,' he shouted, 'I thought you were mad, but
now I know you are the maddest man I have ever
seen or heard of, a slave to eccentricity, selfishness,
egotism, and ambition. To walk after dead battles
so that when you are dead it may be said in your
biography, "He followed the armies of some stupid
dead person called thingummybob, the Duke of Wellington, a hundred years after he had gone by." The
conceit and the stupidity of it ! The ignorance ! The
madness ! And even so,' concluded Don Benito,
pausing for breath, ' what's the good of it all to you
when you've done it ? What are you going to get
out of it ? '

'I should think nothing at all,' I said heroically.
'But seeing you sell your buttons perhaps I might
write a book.'

'Madre mia ! Worse than ever ! ' lamented Don
Benito, leaping with desperation. ' I knew you were
mad, but I didn't know you were a fool. To block
up the world with bad literature, to write a silly

description of a silly journey to add to the confusion
of materialism! Don't do it! It is absurd!' he
pleaded.

'Don Quixote was mad,' I said.

'Yes,' he said, 'I have read about him, and he is
rated too highly. Because every one says the Quixote
is good it must be good, eh? But there are very few
who have read the book through. I don't suppose
you have. He was another of the egotists. Besides,
he was imaginary and you are not imaginary. You
are real. There is no need for you to be a fool just
because some imaginary person has been a fool before you. What does it matter to the spirit in man
that you walk to Salamanca or Vigo?'

A mule team strained up striking its bells
fiercely. Don Benito became unexpectedly kind.
He said:

'But I will not interfere with any man or persuade
him. I will abuse no one. You will walk, you will
suffer, you will learn, and, like the prodigal, you will
return to your father and say, "Father, I have
sinned . . ."'

But the gentle pardoning mood was unnatural to
this meteoric person. Speech flared up again:

'But, man! To walk across Spain and write a lot of
mad nonsense about it . . . it is a thing I cannot even
picture, imagine, conceive of, understand, grasp . . .
ay! and as you go on steeped in egotism, humanity
suffers . . . "the whole creation groaneth."'

Then a woman's voice coaxed loudly from the
corner again—it was the same woman, I thought,
round, heavy-browed and sallow, matronly, though

quite young. She began picking out his things playfully. She called :

'Don Benito, Don Benito—when the sermon is finished—have you a little mirror with a stand?' and her laughter tinkled like trinkets in his booth.

CHAPTER VII.

THE HOUSE OF ILL FAME

'*I suppose* you're a Protestant,' said I to Don Benito at last.

'Yes,' said he, 'I am.'

We had walked on to the high ground beside the fort, where were one or two caves, cactus sheltered, inhabited by gypsies. The walls that Soult had had to buy his way through and that repulsed the English many a time before they could master them, would now have repulsed a continent, for they had become the town dunghill. In the heat the town was almost encircled by a belt of sickening stench. I edged Don Benito down from the walls. One had to step warily.

He went on to tell me he was one of some half-dozen people living in the city who had recently been converted to Protestantism by a Scottish minister who, he surprised me by saying, lived in the city.

'But not now?' I asked eagerly, for the thought of meeting some one who spoke my own language cheered me. I pictured cups of tea, English speech smooth as milk after this bawling Spanish garlic.

Not only was the missionary then living in the city, but Don Benito insisted on taking me to his house forthwith. He led me down from the walls among a tangle of white streets as cool as pipes of water, and eventually we came to a house like the rest, iron barred, small, and prison-like. Don Benito rang the bell. A stout, spectacled woman immediately came to the door of the house opposite and riddled us with scrutiny.

'She's looking to see who we are,' said Don Benito. 'This is called the House of Ill Fame.'

There was no opportunity at that moment for Don Benito to explain his observation, for the door opened. I walked down a tiled passage, and was shown into a narrow room looking on to a court-yard of flowers. In the room was a portable harmonium and several religious newspapers. I remember a sewing-machine. A nervous room, blank and on edge. The missionary was away. His wife was sitting there alone. I do not know how long she had been sitting there, but she seemed to step out of a trance and at first hardly to realise I was speaking her English tongue. I think I was the only English person she had seen for two years—for no one ever goes to Badajoz—and she greeted me joyfully.

'My husband has been away two days,' she said, 'I never know what time he will come back.'

He went out into the world and battled with his enemies, slept in rough taverns, lived on wooden sausage and olive oil, while she stayed in that small white house, working too, but worst of all—waiting.

Her thin lips were compressed in long determination; in her stern eyes was the worried glint of that humour which preserves the sanity of the English. She was simple and pale as milk, meekness and obstinacy and silent courage in her long chin. Straw fair, tall and slight, she was the type the Spanish disliked; they prefer the solid bosomed madonnas to our northern ministering angels. She had no illusions about this.

' They shout after me in the street here, " Ah, there goes the scraggy one, the skinny one, the wicked thin woman," ' she said. ' They like an ample sway-ing pot of oil.'

' They shout after you,' I exclaimed.

' Oh, that's nothing,' she said, smiling and setting her chin. Grey eyes like cold water, I saw. ' That's nothing to what we've been through here ; when it was discovered we were Protestants, it was almost impossible to go out into the streets. We were abused, assaulted, and persecuted. We were boy-cotted by the shops. The priests put out the story that we were spies '—the Spaniard has a strong belief in foreign spies—' workers of the devil, that we were immoral and dishonest swindlers. Even now this is known as the House of Ill Fame ! They tried to force the landlord to go back on his agree-ment to let us this house. But we held firm. We have lived down the insults. The shopkeepers and towns-people, who are good-hearted enough though fana-tical, discover we pay our way and are even more to be trusted than their own. The stories of the priests are discredited.

' That does not mean we are left to ourselves. Our every movement is watched. Every hour we go out is known. Once the nuns called when, according to their calculations, my husband was out. They used the well-known argument, " It is a pity one so beauti-ful should be going to hell. We shall pray for you." I told them I needed no one's prayers, and at that

moment my husband appeared. They had the fright
of their lives. " We must be going," they said, very
embarrassed and crossing themselves. " No, I'll
have my say now," my husband said. They never
bothered us again. But they watch us. Oh, they
know everything. You may have seen the woman
opposite come to her door when you came with Don
Benito. She notes everything. She is their informer.'

The missionary's wife fell silent. ' Five years,' she
said, with those years in her grey eyes. What five
years ! An eternity ! When I had been wandering
about the world, believing in the immortality of
youth, travelling from beauty to beauty, and convinced I could go dreaming on from conquest to
conquest, she had been there waiting, through the
fire of fire, summer, fighting the climate, the land,
the savage people, day after day, month after month
of naked heat.

I could feel the slow, aching trample of those years.
' And does the work progress ? ' I said.

' It is slow, very slow. We feel that little by little
the good seed is planted, and as the years go by we
shall reap the fruit of our labours. We have twenty
years before us and, please God, we shall accom-
plish something. Already a few come to our meet-
ings. It is hard to know if they are converted.'
She was glum.

Twenty years more ! Then she lightened at the
memory of a combat. ' They are such fanatics here,'
she said gaily. ' We use the front room as a meeting
hall, and we hold a service there twice a week '—a
room as bare as a cell, with a reading-desk at one end

of it.—' A year ago, at the instigation of the priests, a crowd assembled outside during one of the services and began shouting and abusing us, then threw bottles and stones through the windows. The louder they booed and the more stones they threw, the louder we sang our hymns. You know what voices the Spaniards have. Then my husband went to the door. Just went to the door. Nothing else. And looked at them. They stopped at once and went away ashamed of themselves. The two priests who were in the crowd ran away, too, like crows, into a doorway near by. They never did it again. It was splendid.'

Thin, white, evangelical house. Ascetic House of Ill Fame, clean and scrubbed, with the texts on the walls.

' God is Love.'

' I am the Way.'

' Blessed are they who are persecuted for righteousness' sake, for theirs is the Kingdom of Heaven.'

She looked upon her life. She said : ' We could not do it if we did not know we were bringing them the Truth.' '

The missionary himself arrived that afternoon. He had come spouting through the heat in an old Ford from an expedition into the country south of Badajoz on the way to Zafra. He had taken the car over a terrible road, a steep of rocks and cactus, to a village perched like a bird's nest on a precipice, and which had no church or priest. ' It was virgin soil,' the missionary said, with the Scotsman's slight blush and twinkling of excitement.

' They'll put a priest up there and a church as well before a month is out, you'll see,' said his wife. They glanced at each other. Neither of them used the unctuous jargon of religious people. There was no talk of ' our Lord ' or ' the Word.' The Scotsman had been in the war. For him the war could hardly have ceased.

' Fighting bigotry and superstition,' was all he said, quite bluntly.

But he did not fit in with the common conception of the fighting parson. He was a small, pale man, with nervous Goya grey eyes ; a man slow of speech, shy, but obstinate, combatant.

' They don't like us, but they'll have twenty years in which to get used to us,' he laughed and skipped like a boy.

Almost immediately he insisted on taking me out. We left her sitting by the sewing-machine. I liked him because he said little. I admired him for saying nothing about his work. It was soon clear he regarded the Spaniards with a Scotsman's contempt, souls to save but not to admire. Yet he was immensely interested in their speech and customs. If he loved them at all it was a solid Old Testament wrathful love. He fed his despisal of them on Napier and Borrow. He had the siege of Badajoz by heart as Uncle Toby had the siege of Namur. He was a man fighting Spain and determined to conquer it. He seemed to be bringing them the truth as you bring others the birch.

He took me to the house of a native missionary, a certain Don Francisco, one of those beatific, black-bearded Spaniards, alive with excited wrenching gestures and the words pouring like pitiful water from

his lips. The fervour of Don Francisco was intense.
He was soon telling me about the Sacred Word and
the way to Salvation. Was I connected with the
Word? No! Ah, God gives each his cross. 'Hola,
Ping!' he called his children into the little white
room of the cottage, which had only a table and four
chairs in it. Two little boys came in. Two more
came later. Excellent children, I said.

' Ah, but that isn't all, I have more lambs than that.'

Indeed, in came four more, one at its mother's
breast, a stout, dark, shining mother, who also asked
me anxiously if I was employed in the ' Word.' A
woman, as the Spanish women are, of the mother
earth, having the earth's tawny richness, fecund, and
patiently strong. Warm, slow, and full-eyed mothers
who trapes from room to room in their white houses,
looking in a wordless, animal calm and stupor at
their young, clutching at them and crying.

' Yes, God has blessed us with eight lambs,' cried
Don Francisco. ' Ay, children,' his lips bubbled
over the word unctuously, ' sing a hymn. Come on,
one, two, three, four . . :'

Immediately an expression of fixed pain came over
the faces of six of the children, whose shrill, bleating
voices—for the voices of Spanish children shriek
without sweetness like a sawmill—sang :

' Jesus bids us shine with a pure, clear light.'

Don Francisco, the Scotsman and I left the house
and went to the town gates, where the police, officials,
hangers-on, and water-carriers, shouting in the dusk
about the fountain, saluted us. We passed out on to

the walls, and under the first clear stars watched the sharp jet roofs cutting into the greenish night sky with that knife cruelty of the Spanish twilights. There was the cool music of the acacia perfumes. And over the treeless corn hills of the plateau cried the white avenues, south and west and east. We were alone.

The Scotsman recounted the history of the siege to us. Don Francisco waited patiently with very few interruptions, until he slipped into a pause in the narrative and began to tell me his adventures in the cause of the ' Word.'

For the Bible sellers, Spain can have changed but little since the days of Borrow. Don Francisco told bitter stories that made the blood boil. The foulness of men when they act in the name of God ! Extreme breeding extreme, the persecuted became as bitter as the persecutors. The anger and rage of those stories have happily left my memory, but nothing can make me forget Don Francisco's histrionic manner.

He pulled his hat over his eyes. He struck attitudes. He leapt, crouched, and sprang again, recoiled. His voice rose and throbbed. It fell. It whispered. He acted every word so that we sat on the earthworks of the city as though held by a melodrama.

' One night,' he said, ' I arrive at a village, a small place in Andalusia, up in the hills. I meet a man in the street. " Hola, friend," says he. " What are you selling, what have you there ? " " The Word of God," I say. " The Holy Word which tells the true story of our Lord and Saviour Jesus Christ, the Son of God, which is the only way to eternal life."

" Ay," says the man seriously and interested, " how much ? " " So much," say I. " Give me one," says he, and then up comes a friend and says, " What is all this ? " " It is a thing called the Word of God," says he. " Good," says the other, " it is what I have always wanted. Give me the Word of God." And others come, and I sell nearly all my books. Then I go to the posada. . . .'

Don Francisco, who had been speaking in the high, fluting tones of recitative, now became ominously dramatic. . . .

' And I notice,' said he, stretching out both arms before his eyes and recoiling like a conspirator who has been discovered. ' I feel that all is not well. The Guardia Civil is there. Aha ! I think he has been sent. " Here you, who are you, what are you doing ? " asks the Guardia. " What are you selling ? " ' says Don Francisco in the peremptory, throaty rumble of authority. ' " I am selling the Word of God, as written in the Holy Bible, which is the only true guide to eternal life," I say. (The apostolic benignity of Don Francisco's voice !) " The Word of God ! What is that ? " commands the Guardia. " Do you not know it is forbidden to sell obscene literature ? To the Alcalde and we shall see ! " he shouts '—shouted Don Francisco, drawing himself up to command, an imaginary prisoner. A long pause.

' And I,' he went on softly in grieved quiet, ' I go. The village follows jeering. Already they have been stirred. The women jeer at me. " The old beardy one ! What a wicked beard he has ! " they cry. I am taken in to the mayor. Of course, of course. At a long table are seated the mayor and the parish priest, one of those gross, cunning people, lolling an enormous stomach against the table. Ugh! (shuddered the disgusted Don Francisco). "What is this?" squeals the mayor sternly. "I am selling the Word of God, the Holy Bible. . . ." "Stop!" cries the priest, banging his fist on the table. "No blasphemy! That pornographic book, the work of adulterers and heretics, is forbidden. It is the work of anarchists and enemies of the one true Church. Take his books and destroy them!" "To the prison," cries the mayor, and I am grabbed by the scruff of my neck (Don Francisco rubbed his neck) and thrown into prison.

'I am in prison. "Ay yai!" I sigh. At least we have a bed for the night. I sing a few hymns. I pray a long time. I wonder what will happen next. I sleep.' He paused. Then his finger went up slowly, mysteriously to his ear. 'Then at four in the morning I awake. Ah! What is that? The voices of men. Enter four guards. Well, what? "Get out, you," they say,' yelled Don Francisco, with a shout that nearly made me fall back into the city moat. 'They drag me two kilometres out of the village into a field, and there I am stripped naked, beaten with sticks, and left unconscious.' Don Francisco's voice sank.

'It is true. Five years ago,' said the minister, 'he crawled into a railway station three miles away, and a porter he knew gave him clothes and helped him home.'

Don Francisco was bitterly quiet, recalling that

scene. Then his eyes broke into sudden black light, and he stood up fiercely. ' But by the grace and hand of our Lord, those men were punished,' he cried in triumph. ' " Vengeance is mine, saith the Lord, I will repay." Within a month one of those guards was shot dead in a quarrel ; another was forced to leave the neighbourhood, and led, as I afterwards heard, a ruined life ; the third died in the agony of syphilis ; the fourth—the Lord smote his wife and his children, and he lives there now a miserable man, noted for his unhappiness. I have never before seen the Lord's power so mighty.'

The story of the vengeance of Don Francisco's God left an appalled silence. I looked about me at the cruel, sharp land, a knife against the sky's light. The bell of the Cathedral banged like a prison bell. Little stabbing lights appeared among the heavy roofs of the town. Only the air was sweet and clear, a balm.

' That was the worst,' went on Don Francisco, wiping his forehead, and speaking benignly, gently now, words like healing oils. ' I have been gaoled scores of times. I remember once arriving at a village not ten miles from here—a village where now the seed of the Word is well planted—and being thrown into prison on the usual charge of selling obscene literature. That I had a special permit from the Governor of the Province did not make any difference. That night I felt very happy, and was sure the Lord would deliver me. I remember I knelt down and began singing hymns, one after the other, as loud as I could, for I was so confident. I began with " We are but little children weak "—do you know it ? It goes like this . . . ' he sang a bar or two challengingly on the walls. I was a little ashamed, and looked round fearfully to see if anyone was coming. Dramatically he changed to the present tense. ' I sing every hymn in the book. Well, soon I begin to hear voices outside the prison. A crowd is collecting. I sing louder and even more happily. " Oh, how happy he is, the prisoner," cry the people. " What a happy prisoner ! There are rarely such happy prisoners in the gaol. And listen to what he sings. It is about God and angels. He must be a good man. Strange that such a good man should be thrown into prison." Very soon along comes a well-known man, a liberal and a landowner. " What's this ? What's this ? " he cries. " A prisoner who sings," they say. And then it appears this is a man of influence. " Ah, I suppose it is that dog of a priest who frightened the mayor into putting him in here," says he. And away he goes to the mayor, and in a few minutes I am released. Fortunately, my books have not been destroyed. They are returned to me. I am publicly acclaimed. The priest dare not show his head. The mayor apologises, buys a Bible, and weeps. In no time my books are sold and all my tracts are given away. The Word of God is soon in the hearts of many people that day, and some weep for joy.'

We returned late to the town. Don Francisco left us. The people were walking in the streets under the cool night. The cafés of the Plaza were loud with light and with talking men. Clink, glitter, sips of talk, slam of money. Waiter ! A hearty clap for the waiter. A hiss like a syphon hiss for him. In and out

of the tables, like a dog prowling, is a woman selling
lottery tickets for some hopeless mañana. A fountain of cries for the waiter. Waiter ! Hiss and bobble
of cork, out flies a cork. Chime and twang and pitter
of words. The tongues of the city stirred up into a
syrup of words by the immense spoon of night.

The iron tables were scattered like music in the
street. Brown beer wets them, fingers were pulling
shrimps to pieces, mouths were spiked with tooth-
picks. Talk, talk, spit and talk from the yellow faces
staring like audible moons. Red soldiers and black
priests walked up and down, up and down, black
priests and red soldiers, spit and talk, spit and talk,
the clink of talk among the chiming tables. The sky
was green as a tree and white as acacia with bunches
of heavy stars. A red bus crackled and spat into the
Plaza, engine talking and spitting with the rest.

Black, full-stomached walls swelled above us.
People came out of shadows into the narrow street
light, passed, extinguished into the dark again like
bats unsteadily.

' Good-night. Walk with God,' cried they. God
was on every one's lips. The dogs of the town were
howling and barking at their night fears.

Against warm walls men were nailed like bats—
lovers talking to their dark ladies through the iron-
barred windows. The heat of love in those old walls.
A woman's voice passing over those bars as though
they were the strings of a lute, ' Walk with God.'

Over the earth the sheen of forgiving night. With
God.

The Scotsman and I said nothing. We returned to

the House of Ill Fame. The supper was waiting in that small room, ill lit by weak electric light. The room was quiet, not the tick of a clock in it. The time must have been eleven o'clock. His wife sat there. I could not tell how long she had been sitting there, waiting.

And after twenty years. . . .

CHAPTER VIII.
THE EVANGELICAL FORD

I stayed in Badajoz three days, afraid to begin my journey. Now I was committed to it, I would have given anything to be able to abandon it. The heat flamed, and the prospect of those three hundred miles alone was disheartening : Salamanca, Zamora, Leon—what arid solitude hung between those names ! But while I was struggling with myself and looking at my maps despondently, the Scotsman announced his decision to take me on the first twenty-five miles by car, and to combine business with pleasure by opening one of his evangelical campaigns in the villages on the way. The idea filled me with horror. By one evasion and another I tried to get out of the arrangement, so repugnant to me was the idea of being concerned in any kind of proselytism. Or perhaps I was afraid.

Of all discussions those about disease and religion seem to me the most futile. People enjoy their diseases as they enjoy their religions, but if only they would keep their diseases and their religions to themselves ! I am interested neither in their stomachs nor their souls. You do not expect to make a man accept your digestion ; why should you thrust your religion at him ? Why is your digestion of ideas the only right and true digestion ? There are as many digestions and as many religions as there are men in the world. Let us leave it at that.

But there is no escape. With the Christians on the one hand gathering their diseases together into one anthropomorphic lump and calling the result God, or the will of God ; and the atheists, on the other hand, having as many gods as the Christians have diseases, lumping them together and calling them Doubt, there is no escape. You must listen to the groaning and the yearning. The love of humanity, like other mass-productions, is cheaper, shoddier than the love of men, which is the ancient, satisfying craftsmanship of the heart.

I consoled myself with these reflections as the Scotsman's Ford bombarded along the road north-ward out of Badajoz. We had crossed that brown, high, twenty-eight arched bridge. The city roofs had flattened into the plains. I was nervous about this proselytism, but happy about my broken vow. I had sworn to walk : I was riding. There is an ex-hilaration in breaking a vow, an abandon. For a moment you expect the skies to darken and holy lightnings to wither the clouds. You are like the old-fashioned atheists who thought to prove there was no God by daring Him to strike them dead for denying Him. Nothing happens. Your vow is broken. You are still alive. You are at the bright and promising dawn of a long, unmoral life. There is nothing that cannot be explained ; anything means everything.

The Ford stamped and bellowed on a road that resounded like a sword on the country, and split the wilderness of dark encina—the scrubby, evergreen oak that covers Spain like a beard—with its flinty

wedge of ochre glare. The sky was an infinite blue
dome in which the light of the sun hummed like
myriad glittering insects.

We stopped at the hermitage of the Virgin of La
Botua, who inspires the peasantry for miles around
to periodical devotions, pilgrimages, and carousals
in her honour. Don Francisco, who with Don
Benito accompanied us, was anxious to see the
shrine. It was a cold, bluish place, not very beautiful,
but cold as ice after the heat outside. The sight of
the emblems of popery filled Don Francisco with
zeal and holy rage. He distributed evangelical tracts
to the caretakers—for there was attached to the
chapel a noble, well-appointed kitchen, shining with
pans, tiles, and great waisted jars of earthenware—
and told me how the image of the Virgin above the
altar had been thrown from heaven by God's miraculous hand, and had fallen into the branches of an
oak tree, where a priest early one morning had found
it. (The Scotsman smiled.) A shrine was built
to commemorate the miracle—on the customary
grounds that it was one of the miracles that create
faith, as distinct from those that are created by it !—
and although it might be argued that God had not
sent down the image, who should limit the power of
the Almighty and blasphemously suggest that God
could not have done it ?

'But the peasants,' said Don Francisco, 'do not
bother about the metaphysics of the matter. They
take an acorn from the tree in which the image was
found, and split it open. They show you in the
heart of the nut a little image of the Virgin. But

it requires the eyes of the faith!' added Don Francisco.

The effect of distributing heretical tracts at the shrine was immediate: we had a series of punctures. Don Francisco leapt out with joy as each one occurred, fetched tools, talked endlessly, while the Scotsman did the work. It was a strange combination this of the small, pale, silent Scotsman and the stout, bearded Andalusian, as excitable as a dwarf, both with their passion for converting men. Don Benito, who came with us, would stand shaking his head sadly at the car and sighing. Once—influenced no doubt by the story of the Virgin—he poked a tract into the branch of a tree.

'Ay yai!' he sighed. He was extraordinarily quiet after the day before.

The best road to Caceres from Badajoz is the red main road that follows the shallow Guadiana for some twelve leagues eastward to Merida, ancient capital of the Romans, and which from there turns northward another fourteen leagues to Caceres. But there was a quicker way across the Sierra de San Pedro, a matter of twenty leagues only, and although for some distance there was no road, that was the way I had chosen. Soon we arrived at that place where the road petered out into a waggon track, and from that became a cordage of donkey paths encumbered with stones and boulders, and sinking into profound ruts, scribbling whitely among the trees. It was like motoring over a ploughed field.

'You cannot go over this,' said Don Francisco,

immediately alarmed. The Scotsman took no notice. The car rolled like a ship, the hoarse roaring and exploding of its engine multiplied, the springs yelped at each leap of the wheels. At times the four of us were catapulted to the roof. At times we ducked to avoid the besoming of trees. We climbed into the

heart of the wilderness and were almost pathless. Don Benito was gripping the seat and Don Francisco the door, preparing to make a jump for it. The Scotsman was unmoved.

'How obstinate they are, these Scotsmen!' kept muttering Don Francisco, and other things besides.

Then the cover came off one of the front wheels. The Virgin of La Botua was doing her work well. The tube blew up to the size of a balloon, but Don Francisco let the air out just in time. The missionary put the cover on; we continued a further hundred yards, and, after clearing an enormous boulder, had another puncture. Don Francisco's little stamina had gone. Don Benito went about shaking his head, throwing his arms up in continual shrugging and muttering to himself. The Scotsman mended the puncture, saying: 'Good! Good! We'll soon be there,' as he levered on the burning tyre.

We bumped on, rolling and tossing. Don Francisco, now white with terror, and groaning at each leap and blow of the car, and Don Benito speechless, numbed with fear, his two black eyes seeming to grow larger, then to diminish in size, as each new terror approached and passed us. By our estimate we had another eight miles of this wilderness to cross. For the third time the car struck a boulder and burst the tyre. Don Francisco and Don Benito let themselves down quietly trembling, and without a word they walked off into the wilderness. In a few seconds they had disappeared in the scrub. 'Not that we haven't given them plenty of opportunities,' said the Scotsman drily.

We mended that burst. We were exhausted. Don Benito came back and said he had been following a most beautiful blue bird which was building in an oak. He smiled with the utmost tenderness. There were tears of happiness in his eyes. 'A little blue bird. It is building its nest there, and then it will have a lot of little ones.' His teeth shone.

' Birds' nests,' muttered the Scotsman, wiping the sweat from his brow.

Don Francisco came up slowly and stood apart without saying a word. *He* had seen no blue birds. His beard seemed to have grown and thickened in those few minutes. His clothes were dusty. He watched the car with head lowered. Once I thought he was going to charge it—like a bull. Then I thought he was going to run away. We all got in, and our banging, bombarding progress began again, and the terrors of Don Francisco and Don Benito with it. It was not until six in the evening, after eight hours on the road, and without having had a bite to eat or a drop to drink, that we arrived at La Roca, our destination.

The village clinked with small, hard noises, like a heap of white-hot pottery held in a kiln of hills— white, one-story jars with heavy red lids to them.

We went to the posada of one Celestino Esteban, a large, cavernous building, with a long archway running from the front to the yard at the back, where the beasts were driven and stabled. There was a high earthenware jar of water in the coolest corner. On either side of the archway were rooms, one of which was the kitchen with a log smouldering in its wide chimney corner. A girl was stirring a pot hanging over the fire, and singing in the minor this simple love song :

' Que te quiero-o-o
Ay, que te quiero-o-o
Que te quiero-o-o-o
Que te casas conmigo-o-o
Con una besita-a-a.'

Outside, the air was fire, but in the cool, cellar-like posada it was as if we had plunged ourselves in the dark of an ice cistern.

The innkeeper's wife was a dark, enormous piece of architecture. Her black hair was drawn back so tight that it pulled her eyebrows out of place. Her eyes were black and bright as berries. Don Francisco escaped from us to order eggs. We ate a dozen eggs fried in olive oil. A log of white bread was brought, which in turn we placed against our chests and pared with penknives, as though it were shoe leather.

' To-day's bread,' said Don Francisco, which is the sarcastic Spanish term for bread that is old and hard as timber. Don Benito brightened at this. Wine was poured out—a kind of raspberry wine—and in turn we drank from the one glass. There was no other. It was handed round with great ceremony, each giving place to the other to such an extent that we drank hardly any.

The room in which we ate was whitewashed and had pictures of the Saints on the walls, and was hung and bunched at every corner with dry lace curtains, which made the little room as white and frightened as a wedding dress.

' We're in good company, at any rate,' said Don Francisco, nodding to the Saints, the sight of which fascinated him, and perhaps filled him with a desire to convert them.

' Ay yai ! And I who was nearly of their company when I saw that little blue bird, do you remember ? ' said Don Benito sadly.

' It is good to be eating,' laughed the Scotsman

grimly. There was a dish of tomatoes done in oil and garlic before us. How he scorned these Spaniards.

' Ay yai ! ' sighed Don Francisco, himself remembering the agony of the journey. ' I little thought I would be eating. When we stopped the last time, I was nearly dead. You saw me go away, right into the bush alone ? You know what I was doing ? '—the Scotsman and I exchanged anxious looks—' No ? I went behind a bush, and kneeling down I prayed. I prayed to God. I said, " Please God, let us arrive at La Roca soon and safely, and make smooth our pathway ! " '

' Ay ! Don't speak to me of it,' cried out Don Benito, covering his face with his hands. ' When I saw that little bird, I thought of the holy words from the Bible, " The birds of the fields have nests," at least, you know ? ' The two men went over every inch of the journey, every horror and twist of it, in their conversation, and endured those exquisite agonies and cruelties once more.

' Now,' said the Scotsman after an hour had passed. I dreaded this opening word of his. The evangelical campaign was to begin. How was I to get out of it ? What would happen ? How would the quiet village receive these disturbing men ? Should we spend the night in gaol ? One or two wild-looking peasants came wearily in, well padded with leather, and with black sashes round their waists.

' Holà, friends,' they cried. ' Give us a glass,' they cried. Their faces were lined and grooved like red fields by the ploughing weather. Their eyes shone like bits of glass thrown up on a furrow.

The three missionaries saluted them and went out, having provided themselves with literature. I chose the opposite direction, and went down to a dried-up stream—in winter a boiling flood that rose to the backs of the houses as red as blood. Every one in the village gazed at me. The men were still in the fields, but the women were sitting on the doorsteps in large gossiping circles. They were sewing. As I passed some groups the voices became little belfries of laughter, but others stopped both talk and stitch and watched me suspiciously, with needle in air. Who was I? What was I selling?

I came upon a group of men mending a cart wheel by the stream, dark, lanky, hairy men in steep-crowned hats and corduroy, who were arguing as to whether it was better to put the rim of a wheel on with bolts or to swell the wood in water.

'A good wheel rings like a church bell,' cried one of the men. 'A bad one is as dead as tin.'

Seeing me and greeting me they stopped the argument. In a moment I was among polite friends.

'How are you?' asked the man who knew the true note of a wheel, a thin, cunning, cropped fellow, with big ears poking out.

'I am well; and you?' I asked.

'Very well, I thank you; and your family?'

'Excellent,' I said. 'And yours?'

'Very well, I thank you,' said he. 'I hope your mother and father are well?'

'They are,' I said. 'And yours?'

'In excellent health, I thank you,' he said.

'I am glad,' said I.

Then I told them, in answer to their questions, who
I was, how old I was, that I was married and had no
children, that I was going from Badajoz northward
to Caceres and beyond that, and that I took photographs with my camera.

This pleased them. They were very amiable.

' And is your country a good and rich one like this,
with a lot of work in it ? Or is it like the land of
Portugal, which is so bad that labourers come over
in the summer to work in the harvest ? '

' Ah, those Portuguese ! ' exclaimed another who
was holding the wheel. ' The trouble with those
Portuguese is that you never know if they come
buying or selling, such a language they have.'

' A German passed through here the other day. He
was walking round the world. He went to see the
mayor. The mayor gave him a peseta,' said the
other. ' If you went to the mayor he would give you
one. To all poor, honest travellers he gives a few
pence. The beggars and wicked would not dare to
present themselves. You go, and see if he doesn't
give you something,' said he, rubbing his fingers
together significantly, with peasant cunning, and
winking.

' What you ought to do is to go over to that
country westward,' said the man who was holding
the wheel, pointing with a hammer.

' To the beautiful hills that lie between here and
Portugal. Well, only too well do I know that
country,' he sighed. ' For that's where my three
mules were driven off and stolen only a few weeks
ago, by gypsies. For a week I searched for them and

saw nothing, though the country was beautiful. But,' said he, winking gravely, nodding his head and putting his finger to his mouth, ' there are those in this village who could tell me something about those mules. But I cannot say anything. Patience ! '

The sun that had beaten me hotly as a driver during the day, jumped down, gave the world its last thwack of light and dropped behind the hills, which leapt up black and sharp. The air became quickly cool and sweet with the incoming odours of the barley fields, the sharp incense of wild lavender. From the dense groves, where the stems were budding, was exhaled like a mist the ecstatic perfume of orange blossom. In Spain, when the brassy day has pounded out, flows in the scented music of the dusk, the long anointing coolness after the heat.

I walked away in that wine air, and climbed up alone into the silence of a hill above the village, and thence I looked down upon it. It lay like a bowl of sugar nobs in the hills. As the darkening fountains of the dusk sweetened the sky, the outside silence of the world tightened so that even the clip of an insect was a cry, and the clinking and noising of the village minute orchestrations. The air became aqueous with bells. There were the bells of the goats as they stepped down into the village, stout udders stiffly jerking, bells that twinkled music like stars in the streets. The creatures scattered with that air of learned inquiry into the Plaza, dispersed in the streets, wandered in and out of the cottages, and everywhere they went their watery, seeking bell-music sang, deep now, and then trilling as though every particle of the falling dusk was a carillon and the first white stars clangouring bells above them. The world was melting into bells.

Then came the deeper, brook-pouring of the sheep bells, the bells of the thick, low sheep, who pittered in with a solid world of dust about them, bells that warbled and beaded like spring water aiming to its pool. The sheep kept together, and they moved like a ruffled lake of calling water. And then I heard the slow tolling of the ox bells, as yoked teams came treading with quiet power and deliberation over the lanes of stone, slow as time : Yeats' words,

' The years like great black oxen tread the world . . .'

Dogs barked, one vying with the other, epidemics of barking. Quietness, bells, and again the barking of dogs. The children played, screaming like birds.

I sat on a rock in a bean field listening to the life of the village now almost in darkness. Wood fires were flaring up in some of the yards. There was a big one in the courtyard of the posada. White specks on the gloomed breasts of the hills were women coming home with washing on their heads from the upper reaches of the stream, where the water was still pooled. A form loomed up like tall smoke, like a black ghost inordinately high, moved noiselessly towards me down the path, towered over me—a woman carrying a jar of water on her head from a spring in the field. The little Plaza, which had been empty of all but sun, was now black and loud as a rookery with talking men. They stood about in groups, and sometimes one fluttered gesticulating to another group, as a rook might flop to another bough. The women still sat at the doorsteps talking among themselves. Somewhere in this beautiful, blessed spot the missionaries were selling or giving away their disturbing literature declaring the war of religion. Every new idea is a war : every old one peace. I wondered what had happened to the missionaries.

I went back to the village, and as I crossed the Plaza I saw two men unfolding a tract. As I passed I heard one say, ' It is a joke ! ' I saw no trace of my companions until seeing a large, open window with a yellowish light in it. It was the village café. Going in, I heard words which put things beyond a doubt :

' . . . They come speaking as men with their hearts in their hands, but I tell you they are the same dogs with different collars. The world is bestial, weighed down with materialism, ambition, egotism . . .'

Don Benito had an audience.

I had a clean bed in the posada. Don Francisco slept on the floor, as he was afraid of dreaming about the car ride and throwing himself out of bed. He was, he said, a restless sleeper. The peasants flung themselves down on sacks of straw on the cobbles in the archway. The wooden door was closed. Through the cold night that posada snored, roaring like a den of lions.

CHAPTER IX

AS A HAWK

She is tall, old, and slight. Her head is a hawk. She is tawny, bird taut, and her eyes are bird bright. I heard her voice a quarter of a mile away as I came down the yellow hill. I heard her voice over a field of lilies—the lilies of San Nicolas, they call them, white, floppy, and abundant as country girls—and a field fierce and indigo with lavender. There were the baked red and white rectangles of a village a mile to the west, green hills with red quarries burning in them beyond. There were glassy, rippling fields of green barley. There were heather, roses, broom, and thyme. The sky lolled like a grotesque purple body upon a couch of hills. In the air's fire I could see the dark, sparkling figure of a horseman riding on a track through the lavender towards the inn. The inn was a pink wall outstaring the sun, a bitter wall, a strident wall, and in the centre was a black doorway bored into the glare. And from that doorway her voice queened like a bird's over the valley, darting here, diverting, asserting high, descending quickly like a song, and poising hawk-like, still, holding the valley beneath the lift of its wing.

I am at the posada before the horseman. The heavy wooden door is nearly closed. There is just a slit of blue sky. The room is dark and cold like water. At one end of the room is a chimney corner in which an oak log is smouldering on a heap of white ash

80

where a black pot bubbles. There are two benches
along the white stone walls.

And here she stands, hawk head erect, eyes sharp
as black diamonds, commanding every one. There
are carters and labourers in corduroy, red sashes, and
leather fringes to their trousers, earthy, yellow-faced
men with scrubby bits of beard, all shouting at one
another. She moves from the counter where she is
pouring out little glasses of watery wine, hands
outstretched, holding the glasses. She takes the
ha'pennies. She serves a man who is sitting on the
bench, legs wide apart, red as a cow. And though the
men are shuffling their feet and swinging their hips
and beating their calves with sticks and banging each
other on the back, saying, ' Friend . . . this,' and
' Boy, the other,' her high voice from her old
peasant head, wise as a bird's head, rings continu-
ally and pierces.

The men speak with all their bodies, and volu-
minously fill the room with blurred words and
rumblings. There is the story about Pedro. Every
one laughs about Pedro. To mention Pedro is to
command success for your story. Oh, Pedro, what's
the latest he's been up to ? Oh, you haven't heard
Pedro's latest ? Well, friend, it is like this. Man, it
is like this. They told Pedro to take two chickens
and two young dogs over to La Roca. What does
Pedro do ? Friend, you cannot think what Pedro
does. Man, he sticks the chickens and dogs into
one sack, into one sack, the boy, and the chickens
they . . . and the dogs they . . . well, ha ! ha ! he
was carrying them on his back. And I saw him, and

I said to him, what have you got there struggling ?
I said. You see, it was in the sack, man. Well, he
said, no it isn't a pig. It is the two dogs and the
chickens, he said. And the chickens, he said. The
two dogs, man ! And the chickens, man ! In the
sack, the dogs and the chickens. Ha ! ha ! he
said.

They tell this tale between their drinking, arguing
about it, turning it over this way and the other, and
it fills the room, struggling like the dogs and the
chickens in Pedro's sack. The air is crowded and
jumbled with words, and of course there is spitting
and rolling of cigarettes, and the rest. But it is *her*
voice that rings clearly like a hammer on an anvil.
It pierces. It is direct. Every one notices it.

' Ay,' she says, ' the noblest and simplest heart in
the world has that Pedro. I remember when he was
a child. The best man in the world, who thinks
there are no evil men.'

The noblest and simplest, the best man in the
world they say. The best. The noblest. And the
simplest. More wine. The coloured. It refreshes
more. The best man in the world. Another small
glass ! Have you matches ? Spurt of fire and the blue
shafts of smoke slant among the men like clouds
below shouting mountains.

Her hands are dibble-dabbling in the water, washing the small, weighty glasses. White or coloured ?
White or coloured, she asks every one. Will there
be rain ? This heat, this sun . . . if there is no rain.
' God has sent no rain,' she sings. ' Who knows
what God is going to do ? If I knew as much as God

I could tell you. If the priest can't say how can we ? '
she laughs.

' Clearly ! Clearly ! ' chorus the men thickly. But
her words are like hawks flinging out of the door
and winging over the valley. She talks from her
head only, and it shakes as the words wing out, her
long, gilt earrings stamp and glitter like little
dragons. Nothing more restive, vehement than her
fierce earrings.

There is a banging at the door, the blows of a
whip.

' Patrona-a-a ! Here half an hour I am waiting,
woman ! ' boils a man's voice, and by the sound of it
he is a stout man, with a heavy chin that weighs his
mouth open at the end of his shouts, and his yellow
teeth and his lips are muddled by saliva.

She alights by the door and pulls back the upper
section of it. There is the horseman. His face is as
red as a sirloin. He is perspiring. His steep-crowned
hat is pushed back on his head. He has great posses-
sions of body, and they are divided, as it were, in
panniers over his horse. He never ceases shouting
and complaining : he is one of the masters, a farmer
of wealth.

' A bottle ! I say ! Woman ! How many more
times shall I call. And a good bottle ! A full one,
too ! I do not like your skimpy bottles. A good
bottle of brandy, none of your glasses. What is the
good of a glass of brandy to a man, eh, woman ? '

The labourers fall silent, and turn gaping at him.
One of them is rolling tobacco in his hand.

She gets the bottle and gives it to the horseman,

who lights a cigar, a raucous one, and fires the smoke
of it into the posada, and says there is one thing is
certain in this world, and that is labourers never
work.

'I shall want more bottles before I'm done, woman!'
he cries, and pays with ostentation and ogles. She
claws up the money nimbly. 'Good,' he says,
glowering at the inn and spurring his horse. 'Adios!'
he shouts contemptuously. 'Vaya usted con Dios,
Don Antonio,' chorus the respectful men. 'Vaya!'
briefly says she. She cannot waste a whole sentence
on him.

The door is closed and we are in semi-darkness.
The horseman has broken up the volubility of the
men. Three pay their ha'pennies for the wine and
are about to go. The others stick their hands in their
pockets. She goes to the counter and washes the
glasses, the water rattling and swishing over her
hands, the earrings jumping gaily or swinging with
pointed dignity.

'Ay,' says she. 'It appears to me Don Antonio has
become less formal since he made all that money.'

'Yes! yes!' mumble the cowed men.

She puts the bellows to the log and soon the log is
blazing, and the stinging blue smoke fountaining
into the room with flakes of ash dropping like snow
about. She fries me some eggs in olive oil. I sit on
a stool and eat them.

'I do not like these fantastic men. I like a formal
man, a man of dignity,' she says, walking to the
water again.

Her face is slight and sharp and incised finely by

the sun, grained, carved, cut with the ascetic,
polished graining of old wood. She is dark, tawny as
a gypsy, but no gypsy has her metallic fineness, her
sharpness, nor have gypsy eyes those arrowing,
brittle, shivering lights that hers send out.

I sit there supposing soon I must step into that road
of yellow flint and fire again. It is two o'clock. I
have walked only ten miles since the missionaries
offered prayers for me, and after a score of good-byes
and a hundred promises, let me start from La Roca.
I remember Don Francisco's prayer : that the Lord
would send me a good journey, pleasant company,
welcome wherever I went, and good news from my
wife. In Spain one is not a man but one of a family.
I smile at the recollection. She sees me smiling. She
smiles. She seems to know everything, to have seen
everything as a high, gazing hawk sees into all
things.

As I march up the hill and the pink posada is a
diminishing blaze, I still hear her voice following me
like a bird.

CHAPTER X.

THE VENTA DE LA SEGURA

It was important to attain the next hill, to advance upon the retiring ranges, to attack them, strike through them, and see what lay beyond. To sit and rest by the wayside was to let precious excitement of living and diamond minutes pour through the fingers wastefully. Instead of resting during the heat of the day I marched through it. And it *was* heat : a vertical wall of cerulean throwing out a fire that branded the skin, throbbed in the ears and immersed the earth in a brilliant presence weighing upon everything and silencing it. I would cross the Sierra de San Pedro rising before Caceres, and teased myself with the idea of reaching that town itself, thirty-nine miles from my starting-place.

I knew such a march to be beyond my powers, but who does not play the hero and exaggerate the magnitude and ardours of his task ? I walked savagely in those early days, and men jogging high on bulging mules and donkeys up the long, red loops of road, stared at me in stupefaction and remembered only as an afterthought to say ' Vaya usted con Dios,' the eternal ' Walk with God ' of Spain. I struck trees with my stick, splitting bark, bruising nettles. I sang loudly everything I could think of, and imagined so many adventures that my heart was beating loudly with the rotund excitement. I was leading a glorious invisible army, and each swoop of the road before me rose brassily like a heralding bugle challenge.

In the unheroic moments when I made my imagination admit I could not reach Caceres that night, I decided that in the pass of the Sierra I could stay at the Venta de Clavin, of which a carter had told me. There was not an inch of shade on the road. The sun was riding on my shoulders. Around me camped the wilderness hills, dark as gypsies and, in the great distances, wild ranges waved and crinkled like intense licking flames at the summits. It was as if the earth were a huge pan frying between the curled, violet flames of the mountains.

I was marching through one of those immense uninhabited wildernesses, the despoplados of Extremadura. The sunlight crackled and split and splintered among the oak scrub and blazed spurting like blinding gas flare from the great boulders. Lizards leapt up in vivid rain from my feet, and there were the cries of frightened birds breaking like rods of fountain water among the trees. At the feet of the trees was the common multitude of spring grass, and on it the trees stood in their tilted pools of shadow. One passed walking from pool to pool quietly in the grass like a leaf gliding over the dabbled pebbles of a clear stream.

After some miles I heard the familiar aqueous talking of sheep bells in the wilderness, and at last overtook the outskirts of an enormous flock of sheep babbling northward. There were four huge dogs, like mastiffs, with them, and I saw the shepherd, a weird man clothed in fantastic bits of sheepskin and

cowhide, lichened with age, walking high on
wooden clogs over the turf and carrying besides a
crook and a leathern botero of wine.

We greeted each other, and I walked with him
among the trees. He told me he was driving sheep
twenty-five miles, and would do half the distance
that day. His master then sent the sheep northward
for the summer by train to Leon, so he had only to
put them on the train, for which he said he was
grateful, as he used to have to drive them northward
all the way, on foot.

'And you are walking to Caceres?' said he. 'If
you walk well and if the sun does not get too hot,'
he said, looking up appraisingly at that enemy, 'you
will arrive before midnight. Another eight leagues.
And you have no beasts!'

A man bent up and straddling with the gait of an
olive tree. Forty miles was nothing to him!

He was one of that great number of itinerant shepherds who twice yearly drive their huge flocks across
Spain, spearing the night-black hills with their red
fires and sleeping in huts made of mud and branches.
Creatures solitary and silent as animals. The flocks
spend their winter in the south, where the climate is
mild and the pasturage fresh; but in May, when the
sun empowers himself of the south, they are driven
over Extremadura and La Mancha to the northern
provinces. The custom is an ancient one, and came
to be called La Mesta, and there was an authoritative
Council of the Mesta which looked after the rights
and privileges of the wanderers. Although the Council has been abolished this hundred years, the cañada

de paso or sheepwalk, ninety paces wide, is still left
on either side of the great roads.

It has always been assumed that the custom of La
Mesta originated in the days when the victorious
Spaniards drove the Moors out of Extremadura,
razed and devastated until the region became so de-
populated by the sword and the plagues that vast
territories, at one time as many as fifty districts, were
left unclaimed. It was to these the highland shepherds descended with their flocks and the long
seasonal migration began. Some flocks travelled
between two and four leagues a day. There were
endless disputes between the shepherds and the sur-
viving resident farmers, but the Council of the Mesta
was powerful enough to protect the shepherds. The
Council no longer exists, but as my shepherd showed,
the custom survives, and although he was taking his
flock to the train, most of the shepherds I met there-
after were proceeding on foot, for it was early May
and the northward trek of two or three hundred
miles had begun. It was one of those dust-raising
armies of sheep that deceived Don Quixote. Northward, as I walked, swelled that lake of bells.

At six in the evening I completed my twenty-three
miles at the Venta, a disappointing hovel in a clearing
of the red hills. The sun banged down like a hot bell.
Men in the woods were loading cork bark on to
carts. They gave me water in the Venta, and asked
me the usual questions. Who was I? Where had I
come from? Where was I going? What was my
trade? Was I married?

To tell the peasants I was an author would have

meant nothing to them. They would have considered
authorship a suspicious kind of crime. I told them
I was an itinerant photographer, and that I took
photographs of interesting sights and sold these
photographs in England. But why was I walking?
A train journey across Spain costs!—ay, what it
costs! The beardy, gravelly voiced innkeeper pulled
a piece of bread and garlic out of his waistband. He
knew how much things could cost!

I sat with the family in the yard. I gleaned there was
another inn with the promising name of Venta de la
Segura, less than a league away they said, in the plain
on the other side of the pass. I felt that Venta could
not be quite so filthy as this one, and after an hour's
rest, the sun being lower and the cool lengthening
with the shadows which now pierced the road, I
descended to the plain in which the Venta lay.

A miraculous floor of emerald that plain was with
the road now white—for in the hills it had been
grinding red—breaking it like a sensitive vein in
marble, or a slight line of spent foam in a calm sea.
Young, brief crops of beryl rippled in it. I breathed
the evening ecstasying fields, slender exhalations of
serenity and paradise. Before my eyes the level
swathes of the Vega lay back to the pale beams of the
hills of Caceres, fifteen miles away.

The devil take those cork-gathering innkeepers at
the Venta de Clavin, for there was no sign of another
inn for some miles. Night came quickly; dark,
moonless night and cold. There were no trees, no
landmarks, only the grey dimming sea of plain on
either side of the road in which my feet churned up a

great foam of dust. My spirits began to fall. I had walked twenty-seven miles. My feet were sore, my body was aching, and the straps of my haversack cut my shoulders. Where was the bombast, where was the pace of the burning, golden daytime when I had ridden early over the red Sierra like a gay boat over a sea? The stroke of my heels was now muffled by the dust. I was walking upon a cloud-white path of silence.

Out of the darkness a man tapped by on a donkey. He stopped singing to stare at me, and, when I hailed him, said the Segura was a league away, and that I should know it when I saw it because there were three trees—the only trees for miles and miles—and a ruined tower which people called the Torre del Moro.

At nine o'clock I saw a light scratching the darkness like a pin, but I seemed to get no nearer to it. Left, right. Left, right. Hunger pulling and biting at one like a pack of wolves. Feet burning. I was the only sound in that plain. At last I saw the three trees and the tower, tower and trees, tower and trees, and the forms of the buildings. The light had gone, perhaps it had never been there. The place appeared to be abandoned. There were no windows, no doors. No sound but the crackling chorus of frogs in some pond. Opaque night. Nothing.

The ruined tower delivered its muffled blow of darkness in the face of the star-populated heavens. Not a very cheerful destination for one who had walked about thirty miles out of the frying-pan of the Sierra into the fire of the plain; and talking of frying-pans, oh, for some food. My eyes groped the darkness for sight of door or light, and as I stood there the air was suddenly twisted into the spiralling caterwaul of a peacock. A vulgar, gaudy cry. Where there are peacocks there are men, I argued. (There is nothing so comforting as poor logic.) I felt my way across a mass of rock, turf, and cart tracks, towards the smallest of the buildings, and was rewarded by an open door.

The building was a small stone hut. I stepped inside. The place was in darkness, but I heard voices from a room within. I might have been in a stable or a workshop, for I knocked into a bench with an iron vice on it and came to a couple of stone steps rising to an inner room. A man came out of the inner to the outer darkness and asked me what I wanted.

' There is no Venta here,' he said. ' Though they call this the Segura, because we sell brandy to carriers and to the labourers in the fields. I am the black-smith. There is no Venta between here and Caceres, three leagues away. We certainly cannot give you a bed for the good reason that we have none. We can give you something to eat, yes. If you don't want much, because we are poor people.'

A woman now appeared from the passage with a yellow oil-flare in her hand smoking, hungering green fumes of burning olive oil, that struck the room and splintered it with shadows, like a window starred by a stone. I was in the smithy itself. She set the flare down on a bench and I saw a twitching forge, the shaking stacks of iron, the benches jumping in the light.

' No, there is nothing here,' said she.

She was small, stout, and young with large calf-like gaping eyes, and she wore over her shoulders a pink and green embroidered shawl, knotted so tightly at the waist that it seemed to make a humpback of her. Her candle-pale face was framed in her braided hair, and her earrings jingled and jumped like two grotesque, gilt animals, from her ears.

I took off my pack and sat down on the floor exhausted. The man and his wife watched me anxiously. I asked for water. She brought this. Water cold as swords piercing me. I shivered. Then I told the smith who I was, where I had come from, where I was going to, what my trade was, how my family was, and that I was not a Portuguese. He became very interested and friendly, and was amazed at the distance I had walked, and was very worried at not having a bed to offer me. He told the woman, his wife, to get me something to eat—eggs, sausage, something or other. He sat on the anvil, and his block of shadow wobbled like a fantastic black cloud over the walls. He said perhaps I could sleep with the labourers in the tower. He asked me had I been to Madrid, where the traffic was tremendous, passing, he said, like a flight of parrots ?

The smithy was roofed with boughs of trees. The floor was of earth and cobbles. I smelled frying, and in time the woman brought me a fine plate of eggs fried in oil, and gave me a round of bread as hard as a rock and some water in a tin. We sat talking.

A carter came in. A man whitened with dust, and with curly black hair tumbled in bushes over his eyes, which bloomed wildly through them. He called hoarsely for brandy, and his voice was garlic and crumbled like earth as though speaking were too much for it. He wore corduroy, and leather, brass-studded facing to his trousers. He sat down on the floor and stared at me, biting bits off his whip. He could contain his curiosity no longer. He asked me, 'Has the friend any gold or silver?'

I was mystified.

'Has he any gold or silver, the companion?' he asked again.

'Money?' I ventured.

'I thought the friend might have brought some gold with him,' said the carter, watching my face.

'Ah,' said the smith, 'what he means is, have you any contraband? He thinks you are a Portuguese smuggler, and that you have smuggled gold earrings and ornaments across the frontier, which is so near.'

The smith explained all about me, but the carter was not convinced.

'Many people come over the border at night—it is not too far—and bring gold and silver,' he said doubtfully.

'Yes,' said the smith, and explained again what I did, but the carter only glared, and said it struck him as fantastic that a man should travel from his own country and on foot from Badajoz and not bring contraband. All the Portuguese brought contraband.

We talked and argued till nearly midnight. Then the smith went out with the carter, and left his wife and me sitting on the doorstep.

A taut, clear wind was stretched across the darkness,

and the stars were scattered from horizon to horizon, like the night fires of a myriad shepherd camps on an immense plain. Fires like a multitude of jewels, and when one raised one's arms to the heavens the stars shone like rings upon the fingers. One had the sense of omnipotence and of the incalculable riches of the heart, and again the sense of blackest loneliness. The tower was crowned like a king with a diadem of stars.

The woman sat at the door. She was pretty and tired. Her voice was slow and weary. Again and again she sighed, ' Ay ! Ay ! '

' Are you married ? ' she asked.

' Yes,' I said.

' Have you any children ? '

' No.'

' Ay. No children either. No children. How lonely life is without children. Seven years I have been married and I have no children,' she said blankly. ' Ay ! And your wife is alone ? Ay ! Poor creature, to be alone. And you wander alone ? Like the shepherds who never see their families. What a life for them. Ay, poor creatures. And is your wife older than you ? I am older than my husband. I am two years older. It is better for the woman to be older. Ay, it is better, much better. Ay de mi ! It is better, because thus there is more confidence in the house,' she said. ' Ay de mi ! I travelled twenty miles to-day on a donkey to the market and I am tired out. It is wonderful to go to the city.'

Her husband came back with two big sacks of straw. ' Antonio,' she said, ' he is married and he has no children either.' She looked blankly at him like a pretty cow.

'I am sorry,' he said to me. 'God has given us no children either,' he said.

He then presented me with two sacks of straw. 'I am sorry to have to ask you to sleep here, but we have no bed,' he said. We laid the sacks on the floor. He turned out his two greyhounds and bolted the door.

An old man appeared tottering with a stick at the inner door and walked across to what was evidently a bedroom on the opposite side of the smithy. He looked like the smith's father. The smith and his wife and two younger brothers followed him in, shut the door, and left me in darkness, with polite 'good-nights,' to make the best of a bad job on the sacks, having previously covered me with two vivid red and yellow mule blankets which smelled strongly of their owners. I slept under a boarded-up window near the door. The night was very cold. My limbs stiffened quickly and every turn was agony.

I dozed for a while, but the smithy and its sur-roundings, which had been so quiet a few hours before, now became as lively as the tuning-up of an orchestra. A flock of sheep, their bells babbling loudly, were penned at the back of the smithy ; and near-by was a pen of goats, with bells too, but on a higher, shriller note. The bells of yoked oxen nodded tolling by the tower. Country dogs began barking like artillery, or solitarily howling ; and the smith's greyhounds spent hours jumping up at the door and sniffling and whining around. Little pittering ballets

of mice ran about the thatch and the benches tearing
up paper—the heavens rending like calico—and once
or twice the creatures chased across me as though I
were nothing but a mountain range on the floor. To
add to this minute uproar and dancing, the peacock gouged the air with his twisty cry. I lay
musing. The floor had begun to make itself felt
through the sack, and a host of insects advanced
from the straw and took possession of me like
Lilliputians.

At four o'clock I was awakened most dramatically
out of my stupor by one of the greyhounds, which,
in fury and despair, had leaped at the boarded window
above my head, burst the boards in, and landed
plumb on top of me. In the confusion the beast became entangled with my legs, and though I kicked
him savagely and sent him away yelping, he insisted
on coming back and licking my face. He then
curled himself up on my feet and slept. He kept me
warm. At five o'clock the bedroom latch clicked
up and out stepped the smith. Obviously he had
slept in all his clothes.

' And how did he sleep, the companion ? ' asked
he.

' Beautifully,' I said.

He opened the door and let in a freezing, dawnless
wind, lit the forge fire, and began to hammer out a
ploughshare. Four wild, unshaven men with tousled
hair and bloodshot eyes rushed in and called for
brandy. They had slept in the tower.

' More ! ' they cried.

They drank four glasses each, and then ran for their

lives down the road to the team they had let wander on its own.

Labourers came in and brought ploughshares and pieces of wheel to be mended. The smith and his brother fell to the clang-cling tap of the anvil. The little hovel was showered with sparks and raftered with blows. The woman did not appear. There was no talk of food. The sun was cast into the sky, but the wind was steel cold. The plains were as pale as frost lain to the blue mountains from which, the night before, I had struggled. I saw the buildings and the tower, cold, tarnished blocks of stone.

After a couple of hours a stout, unshaven fellow, a bailiff, for he was not dressed in the peasant leather and corduroy, came to have his horse shod. He was a greasy, yellow man, with a face like a football, almost featureless, and he wandered about complaining about prices, weather, women, horses, everything, with a stained stump of cigarette stuck to his loose lower lip, and his hat planted on the back of his head. The young smith took no notice of him, but sent hard swinging blows arching down upon the anvil. The place rang like a belfry.

A boy brought a bullock to be shod, for the bullocks are yoked for drawing big loads. The beast was put into a kind of stocks outside the smithy, roped down by the horns, and lifted bodily almost off the ground by two straps under its belly, and with its feet trussed by ropes. Two small half-moons of steel were nailed to its hoofs.

Then the woman came out and boiled me a couple of eggs and some coffee, and charged me only two

reales—about fourpence—for my food and lodging.
I made long speeches and protestations of farewell
and, looking up at my enemy the sun, wondered if
I could get to Caceres before he conquered that
country of rock and pink furrows and besieged the
town itself.

CHAPTER XI

CACERES

Mockingly the lead-mine on the hill of Caceres pricked its chimney slim as a blue piston above the plain, and for two hours no stride of mine could bring me nearer to it. After three hours' walking I reached it and crossed the desolation of sheds, stacks of corrugated iron, abandoned rusty boilers, livid ponds, the rubbish heaps, the aimless railway tracks loosed among the sooty, dying grasses, and, after a mile of pink suburb, came upon the ancient city.

Caceres is a small provincial capital gathered about a stump of hill fifteen hundred feet above the sea, like a pyramid of frayed white toadstools. A place of cork makers and tanners, but above all a market and the centre of a region's gossip. Fifteen hundred feet: already I had begun to feel the tilt of Spain's central tableland beneath my feet, mounting like the heat-breathing body of some gigantic animal to the Gredos, the backbone which cuts the peninsula in two. The Gredos were a hundred miles away, four days' march, but all roads like the bones of a vast body lead to the great spine.

The wealthy sense of the south was going. The province of Badajoz enrichened by the touch of blood red Andalusia, had given place to poorer soil. Poorer soil, poorer inns, thinner people, lonelier roads, more derelict towns.

The hotel in Caceres was choked up with commer-

cial travellers, yellow, dejected, unshaven men, who
stood about the passages like jaded crows and spat
intermittently. One, a young man with a tropical
luxuriance of oily hair, discussed the war in Morocco
with me at lunch, and said he had been the chauffeur
of the unfortunate General Sylvestre, who committed
suicide on the battlefield of Anual in 1921.

' Un hombre muy bueno,' said the young man, ' a
very good man,' which is the habitual Spanish remark about the dead. ' Un hombre muy bueno,'
that is subtle goodness, not goodness of mind or
body, but goodness of heart. Spain has produced
more cruel men, and more reckless men, and more
proud men, than any other nation ; and has discovered they are all hombres buenos—when they are
dead. My friend not being willing to discuss the
political repercussions of that Anual defeat, added,
by way of anticlimax that is also Spanish, ' I'm very
fond of photography. I have a Kodak.'

He offered, as a matter of courtesy and without the
slightest intention of fulfilling the offer, to conduct
me to the various historic edifices of the town. He
watched me and listened to me with the gravest
amusement, and though I gave him a brief synopsis
of my life—which every country Spaniard requires of
you—he interspersed nothing but polite phrases.
There was not a word about himself until a chance
remark of mine struck home. I said I had been to
both Seville and Malaga. That innocent remark dis-
lodged an avalanche of local patriotism. After his
love of children and of the sight of blood and death,
the Spaniard's great passion is his native town. The

eyes of my friend burned. 'Ah, you have been to
Malaga and you have been to Seville. Well, I am a
Malagueño, and I must confess Seville is a considerable city. But it is not a port, and it is really a hateful
place. I do not know what foreigners see in it. A
gypsy place, the home of all that flamenco nonsense.
A common place. Tricky, clever, stupid people.
Boastful. Oh, very boastful. Bombastic is not the
word for those disgusting people of Seville. The
gypsy blood is in all of them. How they boast about
their cofradias and the Holy Week! But what are
their processions? The Christs and the Virgins of
Malaga are a hundred times more beautiful, more
artistic, more historical, more valuable, and more
tragic than those of Seville. To me it appears there
is something of the pretty gypsy in those Virgins of
theirs. The religion of Seville is gypsy-like. But in
Malaga we have the spirit of the Mediterranean. Ay,
Malaga,' he cried, blowing a kiss into the air. ' It is a
marvel. And where does Seville get all this prestige
from? How did she get it? Falsely! Falsely! It
was Isabel la Catolica gave Seville its false prestige
by decreeing it the only port for America and taking
from Malaga what was its natural right. Since Isabel
la Catolica did that, four hundred years ago, everything has gone wrong. All the evils of Spain begin
from the deeds of Isabel la Catolica, who is neverthe-
less called by some the maker of modern Spain. But
what did she do? She gave the most vulgar city in
the country an artificial patronage, and ruined
everything. Who were worthier of such patronage
than the Malagueños, who are the most cultured, the

noblest people in the world, and who have the most magnificent processions ? But thus is life.'

He rolled up his napkin from corner to corner, and tied it in a knot so as to reserve it for the next meal. He finished his glass of wine and got up from the table. It was then I saw proof of my conviction that the best part of a Spaniard is his head. The lower you look at him the shabbier, weaklier, and more dispirited he becomes. You start from the full rich hair to the steep forehead, the large, beautifully-engineered nose. Descending to the mouth, where an oily heaviness begins, the lips are thick, the chin heavy, sallow cups with the indigo grounds of beard two days old left on them. The coat is respectable enough, but when your man rises from the table and you see his trousers, the full shock comes. They will be old, shiny, dusty, having no relation to the coat whatever, and the bright red or yellow shoes will be cracked and out of shape from long usage. Spain is a country of fine heads, shoulders of grace, coats that fit the figure, and of anæmic, starved, exhausted trousers. A proud character in slender pretensions.

I carried no Baedeker. I made no routine investigation of the beautiful antiquities the city may have possessed. I do not know what treasures of detail I may have missed : tragic carving, ceilings gloomy with the burden of their beauty, stone and marble on which men have chiselled their desires and then have died. Art is desire, and desire rises in solitude and is consummated among the crowds. Among these I trod knowing only the exterior beauties, the broad

effects and sights, solid harmonies which become
part of the mind as the living of trees and towns and
mountains becomes part of the river that draws them
into its mirror. Above all I was a tramp. A man like
Evelyn, the diarist, who said he did not travel for
the purpose of counting steeples ; bluntly, a man
who arriving under the stout, cheesy arcades of the
town from roads long and deserted, desired not the
solitary beauty but the cacophonous heartiness of his
fellow-creatures. Breathing human architecture, the
tramp sees ; the Baroque nostril, the Romanesque
brow, the Plateresque, faintly sententious manner,
the elaborate, squirming, twisting, belching outpour
of the rococo in conversation, that most voluble of
all styles ; cheeks he sees that are walls of scorn and
eyes that are windows of vision ; walking the streets
the gargoyle and the saint.

The chief thoroughfare in Caceres like Sierpes in
Seville, is nothing more than a paved alley, cool
passage of light, down which no traffic may pass, and
which is almost impassable, because of the throngs of
people who walk up and down it, on their thin and
oily business, in endless, scraping, lisping parade.
Each man is a preoccupied world surrounded by its
own impervious atmosphere. Collide with one,
stamp on his corns, hack his shins, charge him,
shoulder him violently : he will not notice you, he
will not know anything unusual has occurred. So
preoccupied is he with the long yawn of his own
ego, he will not even have felt you. The intermin-
able, spongy cocoon of the Spanish ego. It pleased
me after my lonely days on the road to be walking in

a thronged street and to be cannoning unconscious
bodies instead of empty air.

It being a traveller's instinct to climb to high
ground, I burrowed my way by a coarse lace of alleys
into the old part of the town above the Plaza. The
streets wound up, sly gulleys between the high, cake
brown walls of convents, ponderous churches and
ancient manorial houses, walls plain as fortifications,
broken only by one or two windows peacefully
spaced, or by a broad low stone archway over
which might be the elaborate utterance of a coat
of arms.

The churches were places of large and simple yellow stone, blunt soldiers all of them, with the earthy
Baroque ornament standing out like the veins on an
old, wine-drinking body. The whole decorated lump
was the will of a dogmatic, disillusioned old man, no
high inspiration, but the precious discrimination of a
scholar who had loved the smaller harmonies, the
politer measures. The stern, yet indulgent ecclesiasticism of gold and marble. Churches, sherry
coloured, and pillared churches whose walls breathed
out the heat and were sunken into a yellow torpor ;
creatures, solid and of the earth, matriarchal. The
church is the Spanish woman, the torpid, gazing,
breeding body.

I pushed back the sealing door of one of these
churches and stepped down into the dark interior.
Many people, peasant women and old men, were
sitting in the semi-blackness at the feet of the high
avenue of pillars that rose as though to another
world. At times I could hear, like a ripple in the cold

reservoir of meditation, the mutter of a prayer. The altar shone with a river cave light before which the lean candle flames twirled and fluttered like bright water bubbles upwards, upwards to the mysterious surface in which these kneeling people thought God floated. Church of seductive aisles, hollows of shadow, pooled glooms and sudden lights like fish darting, windows standing knee deep in the waters like miraculously transfigured bodies, naked, and with arms held out in an ecstasy of light—how it laved the mind with emotion and desire.

To descend into the Plaza after the narrow sweetness of the citadel, to pass down under the archway of the old walls, was to come into another world. The Plaza was a long, rectangular place surrounded by the arcades of the houses, fat and white, daubed and scribbled around. During the day the Plaza had not been greatly crowded, but towards six o'clock in the evening, the hour of the great Spanish paseo, the people poured into it in black torrents from every street.

Between six o'clock and ten in every town of Spain the people leave their houses and walk round and round the Plaza in an unending circular procession, the women and girls in threes and fours, the men following them. Slowly and with grace the paseo moves, stirred by the great spoon of gossip, very slowly scraping along the gravel of the Plaza, where the acacias, green cockades tossing, are planted like a squad of sprightly dragoons, the feet hissing, scraping, and scuttling beneath a bird roar of voices. The red and blue soldiers hop about like little mon-

keys, the nursemaids parade in aprons pleated like
opening fans ; and the bandy-legged police, who
have long teeth like cab horses—and look so lean
and lank that they could well be cab horses, but for
the fact that *they* are not taken to bull fights to be
publicly disembowelled.

When the sun quietened and the roofs of the citadel
written above the stocky Plaza were at peace with
gold, the towers broke into a shout of bells, bombarding, barking, bawling a medley of threats,
prayers, and hours like gypsies in dispute. Down
the streets ran boys and women shouting the evening
papers, and they roused the voices of the other ven-
dors to opposition, the bootblacks, the orange seller,
the seller of churros, and the woman, stout bundle of
screams, who cried lottery tickets : ' Sale mañana !
Mañana sale ! ' To-morrow you may be rich. Buy
this, buy that. Pan y toros y mañana sera otra dia.
Bread and bulls and to-morrow will be another day.
That is all it will be, this hoped for mañana, another
day, another like this. Gaudy cries, the earth shaking
on its axis.

Peasants, having stabled their donkeys and mules
in the paradors on the outskirts of the town—Parador del Paraiso, Parador de la Esperanza, Parador
del Sevillano, the inns of Paradise, Hope, and the
Sevillian, not to mention the ruinous church of the
Espiritu Santo, where a congregation of asses and
mules now sing psalms and responses that are nowhere in the mass—peasants arrived on limbs stiff as
poles and planted the red stares of their faces in the
Plaza.

A party of gypsy women, bare-footed, lithe and
tremulous of body, as the silk they wore, and with
eyes as sly as Spanish dogs, shuffled up quarrelling,
running from side to side and picking up cigarette-
ends. Passed by the heavy, white-slippered women
of Caceres, dressed in black, hatless, brown as
churches, eyes black as hurrying, winging priests.
The officers of the garrison came out of the pink
academy on the hill, and stood about like boxes of
bright hydrangeas.

I sat in one of the many taverns under the arcade of
the Plaza, and there was a group of peasants, full
stomached men, with foody, windy voices, who
played cards dramatically for a while and then
talked. They asked me who I was, where I had
come from, where I was going, what I was selling—
the usual questions. The stoutest of them having
disregarded my answers, asked me, ' Are you the
German who is walking round the world ? '

This question developed an argument about the
foolishness of walking, the heat of the year, and a
dispute about the relative sizes of Badajoz and
Caceres.

' Caceres is better for trade.'

' But Badajoz is richer.'

' Caceres is poor as a province but rich as a town.'

' Badajoz is rich as a province but as a town—
nothing, nothing.'

The crowning argument came from the tavern
keeper, a lean, stork-like man who spent the day
pacing up and down with his hands behind his back,
and who crackled a volley of words at the peasants as

he passed them : ' Caceres is more historical and yet it is more modern. It has a cinema.'

The stout man, smiling from the stomach upwards, and with great philosophical diffidence as though he were clipping a fly off the head of a civil governor, cried, ' What life there is to be seen in the cinema !'

At this the street door opened and cymballed, and a tiny fellow, wearing glasses, and who carried a red and green saddlebag on his shoulder, came carefully down the steps into the tavern cellar and, peering at all of us as though we were mere bacteria, let off a question out of his pop-gun mouth : ' How many pharmacies are there in the town ? '

Every one shouted at once. ' There is that of Gimenez Lopez, Garcia, Lorenzo Gonzalez, and . . .' That poor man was given the name of a score of pharmacies. Pharmacy and barbering are the great trades of every Spanish town. In every white alley I saw the barber's brass bowl hanging outside his booth and saw the pharmacist's pestle. Figaro, Figaro. . . .

Dinner was at 9.30. But at nine there was no sign of it, nor at ten o'clock. The little hotel was deserted by its servants and its guests. Every one was in the Plaza, shouting and arguing, gesticulating in the whirlpool. I bought a newspaper. It contained nothing but the edicts of the civil governors—a country, as Unamuno says, of pronunciamiento— the official list of appointments to office that all those groups in the cafés were arguing about, a robbery by a gypsy, and a column about a Sisterhood of the Sacred Heart. But blackening all was a great array of In Memoriam notices in wide borders, with deadly black crosses like the symbols of a suicide club and, underneath, a copious list of the deceased's relatives. Phalanxes of relations. Cousins, nephews, brothers, sisters, in-laws of all degrees. In Spain a man dies that the names of his relatives may be published, and the In Memoriam notices provide the Spanish newspapers with their largest advertising income—and their surest.

The lights were lit in the dining-room at last, about 10.15, the tables were piled high with the plates of half a dozen courses, with the lunch-time napkins knotted and placed inside the soup plates, and a black bottle of wine standing in the middle of every table like a monument.

The strange provincial people who stay in these hotels—though I suppose no one was stranger than I, for that matter—took their seats, talking at the top of their voices. In a moment the quiet room was in an uproar. There came a wide, frog-like man—he had the low, yellow, porous forehead of a frog, the wide mouth rising to the ears, and a way of croaking. His wife and daughter came with him. They were all enormous, croaking frogs. They flowed. Their abundance dwarfed the table. They leaned over the soup, and when they smacked their big lips, leaned back and coughed at one another across the table, the soup had gone. A waiter—a sardonic, familiar spirit—brought them lentils. We all had lentils. But the frog-like father spent the whole of our lentil period in showing his daughter, in foody explosions, how to eat lentils.

'Like this. Bread in one hand. Fork in other.
Shove. Shovel. Rush the heap up to your mouth.
Ah! Nearly in time. No. Por Dios! Try again.
Now, again. Bread in one hand. Like this. Now.
Ya! Like that! Plough the plate. Up now, a
fork full with no drip, up, like that. Ya! That's it.
That's it.'

Three very tall, distinguished, white-haired old
gentlemen appeared at the door together, quietly. It
was like that picture of the Princess Victoria receiv-
ing the news that she is now Queen. Each wore a
slim tail coat, a high wing collar, with a black stock
and a pearl pin winking in the middle of it. Each
wore a white button-hole. Each was grave. Each
was aquiline, the nose aquiline, the chin, the forehead, the eyes, the eyebrows. The silence they had
brought under their arms and spread about the room
was aquiline. There occurred in the face of the
leader, and perhaps the elder of the three, a slight lift
of the eyebrow, which the waiter noted. Ah,
señores. Here. This way, here. Señores. Immediately. All talk ceased. We watched them. We stared
at them. We forgot them. We were lost in thought
again.

They took their seats. They put their elegant
elbows on the table and rubbed their long ashen
hands together, and turned their heads to one
another simultaneously as though they were one
person reflected in two mirrors. At this appeared at
the table a younger man, a man of about thirty. He
might have been a nephew. How he got to the table
no one could tell. He appeared. He appeared as

though he had been produced in sections and fitted together from the pockets of the three distinguished strangers. The nephew—yellow and dark and heavier in the face than they—put his younger elbows on the table too.

' Ay yai ! ' he said, ' I think I shall . . .'

None of us heard what he was going to do, but it did not matter. He would never do it. He would never do anything. Those three distinguished gentlemen turned their faces on him, eyes pounced upon him like six eagles. They held him down. There was a babble of old voices and the explanations of a young one. Lentils were brought. Whatever it was, those three distinguished gentlemen decided that the nephew should not do it. For his part he shrugged his shoulders. He stuck a toothpick into an olive and began to munch it. He spat out the stone. There was a complete silence in the dining-room. We filled our glasses and gazed into our plates.

The reek of the olive oil advanced out of the kitchen. We had cod. Oil fumes crept everywhere, grasped us like green serpents. The skin of the Spaniards began to warm and glisten. Came a tall, emaciated man clearly not of the town, a man from Madrid or Seville, and very disdainful, as though he had never dined among such a horde of provincials in his life before, and with him was a dark woman, dark as an Arab, cloudy face, grape eyes of the half-caste. Every one in the dining-room dropped his spoon and whistled loudly. That started the talk again. Some exclaimed audibly, ' Ay, la mora ! ' They smiled and rolled their eyes. They winked at each other. Quite unknown to her young man she rolled her eyes and grinned broadly at every one. She began to talk to him with animation.

'Ay yai,' we murmured. 'This was splendid. Splendid. Ay yai, where did he pick that one up? Man!'

The nephew stopped eating and sat with his mouth open staring at her. The uncles were too distinguished to notice. Conversation had by some common miracle sprung up again.

Paella was brought. The youth came round with the long, fuming dish on his arm, a mountain range of rice, shellfish, bits of veal, chicken, pork, peppers hot as a volcano, yellow as mustard, dense with oil.

'More, more,' cried the frog-like man, sliding a good part of the food mountain on to his plate with a fork. 'It's good is paella. I remember eating a paella,' said he to his wife with a soupy smile. 'Do you remember the paella we had?' Her face buckled up into smiles. Her bosom smiled. Her waist expanded. She shifted her feet under the table. They all shifted their feet; all those legs knotted like heavy roots under the tablecloth. Did she remember that paella! But none except the frog family was thinking of paella. The question was: 'Where did he pick her up? Ay yai, the Arab. The beautiful Arab. Ay yai.'

The three distinguished gentlemen ate in silence. The nephew as though he did not belong to them. He shovelled up his paella in three blazing mouthfuls and then began picking up his bread and dropping it, staring at 'La Mora.' Hombre! Man!

Between the paella and the veal cutlet every one
stared at her. She was immensely pleased. The man
as hard and thin as a knife took no notice except to
look at her hat and her gloves for a moment. Between the veal chops and the roast beef and salad,
between that and the custard cake, between that and
the biscuits, the cheeses, and the oranges, which
were very dry, because they were out of season, the
nephew watched her. But she who had small hands
like dark silk ate very little in spite of the lolling
voluptuous rondeur of her body, and her beautiful
eyes empty as the bloom of night.

Her guardian leaned over the table and looking
deeply into her eyes said three slow words. She
looked up, and turning ran through a gamut of
laughter and glances. Her laughter and her glances
threw invitations to all of us. Then the mysterious
couple, who had scarcely spoken a word to each
other, rose and walked to the door. The roll of
those full dark hips! Twenty men dropped their
forks and sighed and exclaimed, except the frog man
who had had his back to her, and was now chin
deep in custard. Put your napkin in your neck
then, sloish, when you spill your custard, sloish, it
doesn't soak your suit. The mysterious couple had
left the room.

' I,' cried the nephew, putting down his orange and
starting half to his feet, ' I am just going to . . .'

Oh no, he wasn't. The three distinguished gentlemen pounced on him again. Oh no. Oh dear me
no. Pounced on him. Held him down with their
beaks.

Outside the crowds had thinned away to a few loud voices. ' Sale mañana '—Drawn to-morrow, cried the lottery woman standing alone under the electric laden trees watching the cafés. No one bought from her. Between then and that mañana of hers for which her customers were resignedly waiting, the stars and hours had built up the blessed interim of night.

CHAPTER XII.

THE GERMAN WALKING ROUND THE WORLD

I left Caceres on Sunday morning in a fury because the hall porter of the hotel—but that is too good a name for him : he was a weedy, spidery, hairy individual, who sat on the doorstep with a cigarette stuck to his lip, a man who had not seen soap, water, or razor for weeks—because this fellow accused me of running away without paying my bill. My flood of anger brought down a mass of eloquence with it : I do not recollect ever having had such a mastery of the Spanish tongue as I had at that moment. Subtle idioms and distinguished oaths poured from me. Skilfully, like a canoe, my tongue passed over the deeps and rapids of the majestic Castilian language. That moment of complete mastery was elating and magnificent. I marched into the streets triumphantly.

The stares of the populace did not worry me ; if I had left in a pretty equable temper, I should have cringed before their gazes. The sight of a man in old tweeds and carrying a pack is enough to set a Spanish town agog for a week. On one occasion in the Asturias some friends and I were escorted into the town of Llanes by a mob of fifty yelling children and grown-ups who did not hesitate to throw stones at us and batter at the hotel door with sticks. In Spain one cultivates insensibility. One stares. One stares at men and women. Above all one disregards the feelings of women for they are there to be stared at, and they enjoy it. As I marched out of Caceres in my anger, I gave back stare for stare, with all the contempt of the midlands and the south, East Anglia, and the Welsh mountains, Cornwall and the two bitter parts of Ireland in my eyes. At the end of the town I was stopped by two Guardias Civiles, handsome men in green, yellow, and red uniforms, the finest corps of gendarmerie in Europe.

I expected to be asked for my papers and to undergo a cross-examination. But the truth is the life of a Guardia Civil is a lonely one, and the poor men who police those deserted roads want some one to talk to ; the Guardias wanted to know :

Was I the German who, according to the papers, was staying in Caceres and was walking round the world for a prize ? They insisted that I must be that German. That I must be walking for a prize. For what other reasons could a man walk ? Innocent smiles passed over the Guardias faces like wind over golden corn. I said, to convince them, I would show them my passport, but they restrained me with the greatest courtesy.

' No ! ' they said, ' why should we wish to see your passport, for you are obviously a man of means and leisure who goes as he pleases, and not one of these begging malefactors.'

Ah, ha ! thought I. Tell that to your pernicious, hairy, dirty, old spidery porter in the town.

My virtue thus publicly proclaimed by the police— for we were standing at a cross-roads and a little crowd had begun to gather—I continued my march,

descending a long avenue hill of eucalyptuş from the
town and making hour by hour across a plain, flat as
a table, pale, wide, and limpid as a sea in a rippleless
dawn merging into liquid blue of the horizon mountains.   White farms were dotted at great distances
apart.   Besides the eucalyptus avenue under which
the warm road lay, there was not a tree to be seen
within twenty miles or more.   Portugal to the west,
the rising interior of Spain to the east, as far as the
eye could see the lucid plain lay still under the
ascending ball of the yellow sun.   The sky was high,
wall-less air.   Never had it been wider, more inex-
pressibly far above me.   I was breathing and drinking
that miracle of sapphire, living and walking in it.   I
lost all sense of my body, became an ecstatic mind.
The air was light as though it were being breathed
down from the windows of those cool palaces
whence the winds are fancifully trumpeted.   As I
walked singing I became aware of blue shapes of air,
mountains, snow tongued, to the north.   The first
sight of the Gredos, so far and unnatural that they
might have been no more than the grouping white
smoke of a bush fire in the plain.

Preparing for the north, the cornland dropped away
and the ground rose into a rocky plateau of veldt,
poor pasturage for sheep and goats and herds of
black pigs.   The earth was tumbled with great rocks,
rising to higher, darker bastions on the near horizon,
where, after a dramatic break at a jagged indigo wall,
they rose more wildly, romantically again in golden
madder, tossing and crawling like purple flame.   Beneath the nearer height flowed the Tagus.   Having

breathed the infinite, I vowed to cross the Tagus
that day. But what finite things our infinites are, our
pretty little infinites ! The rocks now whelmed to
the road and shut out all great distances, mounds and
hills of rock, brown coarse lumps emptied pell-mell
over the scanty earth, and the white sheep-tracks,
starved and shrivelled tendons among them. The
heat began to strike like the long hammers of a
million stone breakers upon the rocks. Hunger began to claw, and it is difficult to envisage the infinite
on an empty stomach. I damned that road. I could
see it curled like a bleached serpent skeleton among
that endless panorama of agglomerated rock. At
last I saw two trees some miles away, and a white
house. A Parador.

I dropped on to a stool in the Parador after an hour.
It was a white one-story building on the road, with
a wide archway propped up by tree trunks, and a
roof of new red tiles. It was built of big lumps of
that awful rock and was whitewashed. There was a
small counter and two benches. Nothing more. And
the house was open to the road, for it had no door.

One's first step in a Spanish inn, after saluting the
people of the house, is towards the water-jar, a large
earthenware jug standing in a corner with a dipper
on top of it. There every one goes to drink and says,
' What good water this is.' And it is good water.
There is no purer, more lyrical water than the water
which falls out of the sky of Spain. The Spaniard is
no great wine drinker. He is a frugal man—the
closeness of even the wealthy Andalusians is prover-
bial—and on the central tableland of the Castiles, his

spirit has the arctic hardness of his land, frugal with
his ha'pennies—he reckons all his accounts in
ha'pennies—with his bread, his wine. His religion
is the melancholy mysticism of the half-starved ; his
dignity, the dignity of a nobleman driven to provide
only for his barest daily needs. Eat to-day and let
to-morrow take care of itself. Pan y toros y mañana
sera otra dia.

No man tramping the roads of those yellow and
sepia tablelands under the sun, and in that fine, high
air, wants to dry up his parched throat with Spanish
wine, which is as tart as vinegar anyway, or to add
the lead of alcohol to his limbs. The only drunkard
I saw after considerable travelling in all parts of the
country, was a woman who, in the main square of
Badajoz and on the church steps, began publicly to
undress, to the awe and delight of the children of the
town, but to the natural consternation of the police
and the priesthood.

There is a strengthening harshness in the coarse
blood of the vine, but I desire the silver blood of the
earth. The water that descends from the heaven in
sishing downpour and blends its life with the soil,
that brings body to the lakes and eternal being to the
rivers, a thread of which can split a mountain, a
flood of which can devour a city, a fount of which
cries beading into its pool like a lark, which in a
month mists hedge and tree with the emerald of
spring—that water is good enough, perhaps it is too
good for me.

At this little white Parador I could get no more to eat
than I ever got : two eggs fried in olive oil—ya !

the green stench of it—bread so old and hard that on one loaf I broke my penknife ; and a bit of white cheese made with water and quite tasteless. Menu for a twenty-five miles' march : two hard-boiled eggs —coffee and bread if I were in town, neither if in a roadside Parador—at 7.30 a.m. ; two eggs fried in oil, and bread for lunch at 1 ; two eggs fried in oil, and bread for dinner at 9 p.m., and perhaps a chunk of chorizo hard as timber. In the end a man lives and sleeps in olive oil.

There were two hungry men putting down a new stone floor to the Parador. They crawled about the place in their floppy corduroys and canvas slippers, hot, brown, and beardy creatures who stopped every few minutes to wonder ' if it is the hour yet,' and to make another cigarette. At last they laid down their tools and talked to me, and one of them told me he had known a most beautiful girl who was the daughter of a man they called the ' ingles '—the Englishman—a glazier, that is, a maker of glass, he said, who lived in the province of Toledo.

' And,' said he with great earnestness and fire, ' I would have married her. I would have married her but for the fact that I didn't, and found myself married to some one else, the daughter of a tanner in Casar de Caceres, and now I have two children and hope to have more. Now,' said he, ' does one eat well in your country ? '

It is the perpetual question of hungering Spain. ' Does one eat well ? '

' Ay,' shouted the other plasterer. ' Is it the hour yet ? '

'No,' said the woman of the inn, firmly. 'The master has not yet come in.'

They scowled at her. They glowered like two wild beasts, with the mortar wiped on their faces and their hair hanging down into their eyes, from kneeling on the floor.

'I'll tell you where to stay in Plasencia if you want a Venta or a good Parador there,' said one. 'If you go to the Sevillano you will pay more and get a lot of courses. But at the Paraiso you will pay less. You will not get so many courses, but they will pile up your plate so high that in the end you will eat just as well. At the Paraiso one eats, man. One eats!'

'One eats! Yes!' shouted the other plasterer, the wilder of the two, who slouched about with his hands in his pockets, sultry eyes in storm. 'That's what a married man doesn't do. But a single man, yes. He comes and goes where he likes, he keeps all his money to himself. Can eat and drink how much he likes. If I had wanted I could chuck this game now and be off on the road with you anywhere, Madrid, France. It doesn't matter where.'

'I wouldn't,' said the other plasterer, taking a glass of wine from the counter while the woman was out of the room; 'I'd stay here. There is no place in the world better than a man's own land.'

'Phaugh!' cried the other scornfully, and spat through the doorway at least ten yards, and stared calculatingly at the mark.

The master came in, a tall, old, flaccid man, with a stomach that was doubled in appearance by the wearing of a huge blue sash, out of which he pulled a hammer and a loaf of bread.

'It is the hour?' cried the two plasterers jumping up from the floor like two mastiffs almost with anxious tears in their eyes.

'It is only twelve. Get on with it,' said he.

'It is one. The Englishman says so,' cried the plasterers.

'It is twelve by the old time.'

'But it is one by the new.'

'I engaged you by the old.'

'Ay, man,' shouted the hungry ones. 'Hombre! You engaged us by the new and make us work to the old. The old uncle!'

They flung down their tools in protest.

An argument of arms, hair, eyes, teeth, bodies, followed. The master took no notice, and walked off with his hammer. They stared at each other in hate.

'Ay, madre mia! Barbarity. What a man! What a brute! What an atrocity!' they cried at each other. Sighing, they flopped to the ground and sitting back against the wall, tightened their belts and rolled cigarettes.

'It will look well this floor,' said the one plasterer, looking affectionately at it.

'Yes—when it is finished,' said the other, smiling tenderly and half-closing his eyes as he tried in vain to visualise that remote unheard-of day.

I arrived at the Tagus that evening. At this point the river is imprisoned in the tableland, and like a sword splits a steely way through the rock-armoured land, through incised and sculptured gorges. Battling Tagus, now gold, now steely, cutting its way across Castile and Extremadura through Portugal to the sea. This harried and unnavigable river could have no better name than Tajo, a rent or gorge, though chroniclers say Tajos was the fifth king of Iberia, and gave his name to the river; and even more fanciful men say because Dagon was a fish, the Tajo was named after it. We know its course is a torture, 2000 feet above the sea under summer's drought and winter's ice, and that the stream does not begin to fall till after conquering the high ground about Toledo, it descends as the tableland makes its slow tilt from the Sierra de Guadeloupe towards Portugal. The Tagus, the Duero, the Ebro, the Guadiana, and Guadalquivir are the rivers that do not dry up in the summer; and the warrior among them, the Iberian king, is the Tagus.

The river came round a wide bend out of one gorge, opened into a narrow valley of barley fields and cut like a scimitar, resounding like steel over a low weir, into another mass of rock, and was a quarter of a mile wide. The only bridge over the river was a single track railway bridge, stretched like a gigantic trellis of steel, which took the water at a considerable height. There was no road bridge. Road travellers were expected to go across by a rowing-boat.

I was very tired, and my right foot was so sore that I had gone lame. I was white with dust. But I had vowed I would cross the Tagus that day, and I thought nothing would be more ignoble than crossing by boat when, gloriously, triumphantly I could trespass on the railway. In England we are brought up to respect our railways : they are digni- fied, private as a carriage drive, respectable as the police. In Spain the railway is public, familiar, a thing treated no better than a mule or a donkey that every one can ride on, kick and beat as he wishes. The trains are as slow as oxen and as rare as eagles. It is far less surprising to meet a cow or a flock of sheep or a few pigs or chickens on the line than a train. The poor, soft, smoky trains straining like straggling, exhausted mule teams over that golden country.

I began my trespass, but before a few yards were done regretted it. There was a plank pathway two feet wide to walk on, old, bending planks, and a doddering iron hand-rail nearly as high as my shoulder. That was all. The height and prospect terrified me. There was no railing on the other side, and the track itself was laid on sleepers only, in be- tween the wide spaces of which—wide enough, I thought, for a man to drop through—shone the profound river. Great fears seized me. I felt any moment I might slip under that hand-rail, or that it would break in my hand and I should drop into the river far below, vainly grasping an iron rod. I was nearly half-way across and had not dared to look up, when the sight of the river began to hypnotise me. I saw the bridge was drifting, swinging rapidly away down stream. The far yellow water channelled powerfully against the piers, dividing and opening into a fan of silver rapids and carrying the bridge along with it. I clung to the rail. The water was

uprooting the drifting piers and capsizing us, and
the bridge was already rolling like a boat, tipping
lower and lower over the crawling, yellow currents
and spinning eddies, swinging like a long chain of
steel across these waters. In a moment the sickening
iron would swirl away to nothing. Dizzily I looked
up at the sky, far ahead down the swift vista of rails
to the ochreous cliffs of firm land at the end of it and,
as I looked so far ahead into permanence, the swinging ceased, the bridge righted itself, drifted no more
and rose back to its old, great height above the
water, and as I walked rather breathlessly, now picking a nervous way among the broken planks and
avoiding the wide holes where the planks had fallen
through, I saw the golden bed of the shallowing
river rising like a face out of the dark water and then
the shingles and banks themselves, and so arrived
safely at the other side. I am not ashamed of my
fears for they are my adventures.

I continued my march beyond the Tagus, following
the road to the banked hills of the far side, the road
ascending to a pass. I stopped at a Parador where a
woman was baking at an oven of clay in front of the
house. There was a great number of peasants and
children, and my arrival caused the customary excitement. I sat on the doorstep and was riddled with
questions about myself. The general idea was that
I must be the German walking round the world. The
camera became the great object of interest. Did I just
pull the photographs out of the machine, already
taken and printed ?

The Parador was on the edge of a large field of

barley, still and light-thronged, green as grass, shimmering to the edge of the Tagus. I was advised to go and see the old Moorish tower and the ruins of the Roman bridge, where a great amount of gold and treasure had been buried by the Moors—los moros, mysterious people. I limped painfully through the barley to the river and sat under the ruined pier of the Roman bridge bathing my feet. The long body of olive water played upon my feet, uttering the bird noises, the low throat cries of pouring water. It was not sweet water, nor clear water. It was strong with an edge to it like wine, refreshing at first and then rough as a beast's tongue, with the silt of brassy Castile. Glorious foreign water laving my spirit, too, with its passionate strangeness, bathing me in its great distances, that even now I can feel the motion and the pressure of that livelier being in my mind, winding out of the mysterious origins of thought.

The sun went down. The Parador was a cabin with two rooms. It was certain I could not pass the night there. In time the station-master came across the barley fields from the little pink halt standing stiff as a wooden sentry fixed to a block of platform. He was a stout, elegant man, gold braided, brushed and creased, who walked with his hands in his trouser pockets, a light step as though, with his small, neat feet, crossing a ball-room. He was a native of Toledo and was very superior about it. Don Juan, the peasants called him, familiarly and yet respectfully.

' Well, Don Juan, what's the news from your railway ? I say, Don Juan . . .' as they sat in the dust chuckling, arguing, rolling like so many chickens in

corduroy. His manners were impeccable. For a
long time he could not demean himself by permitting
the indignity of curiosity ; but it was more than
flesh and blood could bear. He encircled me, now
near, now far, like a rotund and shining bumble bee ;
he eyed me from one side of the Parador and then
from the other. He hummed about me, to and fro.
In the end he came up and his question settled on
me : Was I not a German walking round the world ?
No ? His face was a pained moon. He rose, stomach
humming with disgust at being so mistaken in me,
in having lowered himself, in having, as it were,
rubbed the pollen of his society on me. But before
he went I boldly asked him about inns and trains.

'Esa gente,'—a contemptuous 'these good people
here,'—'could scarcely put you up,' he crackled.
'There is a train to Plasencia at 1.30 in the morning.'
It wasn't his train. I could take it or leave it. He
boomed away over the sweet white road between
the barley. 'Vaya usted con Dios, Don Juan,' with
the accent on the Don Juan.

I did not know what to do. I was very hungry and
very tired. I did not want to walk another yard, but
there was nowhere to sleep, unless I slept on a sack
of straw, and I did not feel like that. I must have a
comfortable bed that night. It was fifteen miles to
Plasencia. The thought of doing fifteen miles of my
walk by train was seductive in its wickedness. I had
ridden once. Why not again?

The devil now joined in the conspiracy against my
vows, in the form of a handsome young railway
worker who, having finished a terrible argument

about the number of heaps of stone a man was expected to break a day, took charge of me. He wore blue overalls and was smeared with oil. His hair flopped up and down in one lump as he talked. It was now a night heavy with globes of stars. The peasants had retired into the Parador, the oven had gone out. We were alone. Nothing but the adroit violet forms of the mountains above the mist of barley.

'Every one in the world is my friend,' said the railway man, putting his arm round my shoulder. 'I call every one " Amigo "—friend. You are my friend. You shall eat my rice with me. I am cooking rice.'

Anything was better than the eternal eggs and oil. We went into the railway hut, and there was a pot boiling on a stick fire, from which a most appetising odour was rising. Such was my hunger and exhaustion, I think even a rubbish heap would have smelled good to me. He stirred the pot and made coffee in a deep earthenware bowl. He told me he was a socialist.

'Oh,' said I. 'Does your Union bring you out on strike ?'

'Strikes !' exclaimed he anxiously. 'Oh no. We never strike. Ours is the biggest Union in Spain. We pay a subscription of so much per month so that we do not have to strike. We pay our leaders so much to avoid strikes. If they called a strike we should dismiss them.'

He gave me his views on marriage. He told me he came from Valencia de Alcantara on the Portuguese frontier, a place of great mountains, he said, and that

in this country it was customary in marriage for the
woman to provide the furniture, and the man, as
evidence of his sincerity when he became engaged,
was expected to make a deposit of a few blankets.
Not many. But enough. The most important thing,
he said, was to have children, plenty of children.
Women must have children. It was the only thing
that satisfied them. Not only that, he said artlessly,
supposing a woman gets cross and discontented with
her husband and begins to cease to love him, talks
even of leaving him for another, the one thing that
will prevent her from taking this extreme course is
her children.

' It is good to marry,' he said. ' For a woman must
have some one to admire, and a man must be looked
after. I have a wife whom I love better than my soul.
She, alas, lives at Valencia de Alcantara. Once a week
I use my free pass over the railway to see her and my
children. She is very beautiful, my wife.'

Other railway workers came in. The arroz, a black
mess, was placed in the centre of us on the floor. We
then all picked out pleasant and smoking spoon loads
of it and ate out of the one dish. Sometimes my friend
would pull out a greasy strip of dried cod—bacalao—
in his finger, and holding it up, cry, ' See, friend, a
good piece. See if the friend also can find a good
piece.'

Every one put his finger in the search for good
pieces. There were oil, rice, meat, bacalao, and peppers in that mess. And something else. Something
else ! We wiped our spoons on our sleeves and
spooned coffee out of the one coffee bowl.

'He is my guest, this compañero,' explained my friend to the others, over and over again. 'I have just told him, "Every one is my friend. I will share with all men." And the compañero says he lives a long way off, a journey that costs a lot, that costs so much that the Government or perhaps some Trade Union like ours '—he had not been so impolite as directly to question me on this. 'And it appears he is married and has no children.'

'Ah! no children. What a pity. Perhaps the friend will soon have some children,' chorused the others.

'Yes. Without children life is poor and sad and without gaiety,' said my young man. Then, in case I should have forgotten, 'I have told you I am your friend and you are mine. We are friends. Although you come from your country and I from this one, yet you are my friend.'

The men left the hut and went away up the line. I took my leave. I walked across the barley field to the halt. There was a low yellow moon over the mountains and shining in a rim of the river. I lay down on a bench and, in spite of its hardness, I began to doze. Two women appeared—I saw them vaguely as though in a dream—carrying an iron bedstead into the ticket office, with great noise. They dropped the bed and mattress, clattered pails, but louder than all else were their voices. I heard bits of conversation—'came on foot—no, not a German walking— the train—trade—selling, no—but no children. No, no children. Now this way up. Your end—ya, he's asleep. . . .'

It was nine o'clock.

Four hours later I awoke with a start. Something terrible had happened to me. The halt was in darkness, but for an oil lamp burning on the floor by the ticket office. The doors were closed. I was feverish and perspiring. My body appeared to be on fire. My throat was dry and burning, and my mouth—something terrible had happened to my mouth. I seemed to be breathing smoke and fire like a dragon. It seemed a dark and reeking pillar of smoke breath was rushing from me in a solid mass. My breath burned my hand. My mouth was alight. And the smell, the stink. I sat up amazed by the solid foulness of my breath. What had happened? And then I knew what had happened and what the other ingredient in that arroz had been. Garlic! A heap of garlic, pounds of garlic. I had eaten nearly a bowl full. It was flaring now within my body like a demon. I should illuminate all with a vivid light.

Confused, and thinking the train might have gone, I picked up the lamp and went across to the ticket office, and as I lifted the lamp up, the light shone into the office, and there I saw a sight that would have healed a man of all his diseases. In an iron bed, with the clothes thrown back because of the heat, lay the beautiful station-master, his body heaving like a high blue and white striped marquee, and he was snoring like a gong beaten in crescendo, calling every one to refreshments : ices, chocolates, lemonade, even honey. . . .

CHAPTER XIII.

SONGS, DEATH, AND MARRIAGE

Plasencia stands in the high valley of the river Jerte,
a wide shallow stream that nearly dries up in the
summer, amid a mountainous wilderness of rock.
It is a brown city rotten with the sun like an overripe
apple that has fallen among the lumping hills of iron.
Pigs of iron and copper. There is noise in the look
of that land where the very sky is stony. The iron
hills are stacked around the town, and to the north
are the Sierra de Béjar, snow skull of the mighty
vertebrata of the Gredos. The town lies within a
belt of crumbling walls with sixty-eight worn out
towers among them, and a fine chain of Roman
aqueduct marches out to the high rock behind.

A rotting place rising on a sand cliff above the river
with an iron bridge like the full swing of a smith's
hammer impinged on one end below the cathedral,
and with an ancient bridge, a golden trajectory of
arches at the other end. There are slow tiers of yellow and white walls with roofs flat and ragged as
mats ; a skyline of convents, plain and barrack-like,
out for a fight ; and a cathedral sharp as a host of
spears against the sky. Below the iron bridge, under
its landing arch, there is a three-story mill from which
hangs the beard of water.

There are the usual narrow paved streets knotted
about the hills, the usual Plaza and its arcades, the
hundred little trades, the drab, soiled cafés, where the

faded provincial people sit drinking beer or coffee, playing chess in little groups or sitting alone, large tawny moons of silence and digestion. Storks crackle their beaks above the roofs. The convent bells crack hours and hit prayers.

In the heat, all men and animals make for the sight of water. It is Monday, the great washing-day, and the cliffs, the rocks, the river banks for a mile about the town are white with drying linen. There are areas of sheets lying about so that you cannot get within twenty yards of the river without treading on them. All the women of Plasencia are washing sheets, night-gowns, and underclothes in the bubbling green Jerte, now lively as a field of lilies with the snow water of the mountains of Béjar. The water is combed over the weirs to the north of the town and so broadens into a wide sweep along a field smooth as an altar-cloth on which poplars are green candles, with the sunlight burning at their tops and running guttering down their sides. A grey donkey stands hee-hawing there with his tail recoiled like a thick serpent stiffen-ing to dart. Two or three men wade mules across the river, where it is not more than three feet deep, on to a bank of shingle, and in that glaring bank stand as hot as flies, gathering baskets full of stones and emptying them into the panniers of the mules, driv-ing them up again into the town where a school is being built. There is a breeze at this point where the valley has opened greenly between the barrancos and the shaking olive-braided hills. All day long horses and donkeys are watered in the stream.

Between the two bridges and even beyond them

the town is encircled by washing. The women, with
large straw hats over their heads, kneel by the river.
Some merely fling their garment into the river and
pull it out. The conscientious scrub on boards or
between the fists, and a bluish veil of suds is drawn
out by the fingers of the current and floats down
stream, where the water becomes deep and olive.
Again breaking into shallows, it is a talking, living
passage of light over the pebbles, and the singing of
the women is carried over it and mingles with the
chatter, the pouring, the trilling, and swishing. Oick.
Oick, oie-e-e-e-e, the pure whistle and the thin fife,
until the sung words of the women are dark fish
passing from light to light and merging into the
hanging shadows of the ripples, disappearing as the
water deepens for a rush under the middle arches of
the old bridge, and thence, full of body and still,
presses a course into the barrancos. The women of
Plasencia call minor songs among the ripples, and
their voices rise from the live throat of the stream,
lark-like, water-mingling jubilee in the Arab minor.
As the silt is worked off by the river as it laves the
body of the land, it carries away the gritty voices of
the women of Plasencia across Spain to the sea.
Notes and voices like knocking pebbles, jingling
like pence, voices of silver darkness. Songs like the
stream drenching over the weirs or speaking among
the sallying boulders, choruses that divide among
sporadic rapids and turn about gaily in whirlpools,
and dart off once more in the deep olive minor, and
rise trilling again with laughter. Scrub and wring
and shake your white things among the voices of the

water, the voices of the sun, the mountains and their
winds ; plunge the arm into the reflections of a town
that hangs upside down from its spindling shadow
legs like marionettes ; churches, houses, mills, and
monasteries, cypresses and oranges, singing away to
nothing. Each garment a song with a chime of laughter. Sing water, songs spangling like young poplars.
The white songs lie in hundreds on the banks so that
now the men of Plasencia wear songs and sleep in
songs, and the women of Plasencia wear laughter
and sleep in it.

It is a world where songs are water and the earth is
a sun, where sights are heard and the music is seen
with the eye ; where there is no independent being
but each being lies in some other. A beautiful world,
but a grotesque world, a baffling world like this poor
man here who is chasing three pigs. He has been
sitting on the wall half-asleep and hearing the plash
of song and water. An old man—thin man. His
three pigs stray among the washing that is lying on
the river bank. There will be trouble for him and his
pigs if they are caught near that washing.

'Oi, oi !' he calls to them. When he has caught
two the third is out of reach. He pursues the third
and the two escape. So he tries for the middle one
and catches him by the tail—if devils can squeal like
little black pigs !—and now, by all the Saints, how is
he to catch the other two ?

' Sish, sish, sish !' he calls.

'Ya, ya ! little animals,' he cries. A poor man
trying to do three things at once.

' Oi, oi !' he cajoles.

The three pigs scatter, more like three small black concertinas bumped to earth in a music of grunting.
' Virgin, I shall have to run for the little beasts.'
He chases the three pigs to a wall and edges them through the dust and the sun into a corner. What is on the wall but a million pairs of black stockings drying. Perhaps it is not a million pairs, but the wall is two hundred yards long, and is covered by them. Stockings hanging stupidly, limply, ludicrously, as black sausages over the wall, and each with holes that are like leering eyes. They nudge one another, the shambling down-and-outs, as you pass, jostle like casual dock labourers for a job, make jokes about you, split their sides. You think of the legs that wear these stockings, the legs of Plasencia—the thin legs, the straight legs, the full legs, the round legs, the crooked legs, the curved, the bandy, the ornate, the rectangular, the rolling, the graceful, the trunk-like, the lithe. Of all the owners of the legs, of where they live, and how they live, and the things they say— songs and pigs and stockings and a town turned upside down in the water of the Jerte.

DEATH

It is seven o'clock in the evening. Every one is enclosed in the dense white walls of the Plaza except one man, and no one knows where he has gone. There are the red soldiers, the nursemaids, the blue police with their swords. The acacias off duty strolling about. The air as cool as a great blue branching tree. The people are walking up and down the

Plaza in circles, the men together and the women together. It is like a five-finger exercise or a very slow chattering roundabout. There is a cheap Jack selling earrings, razor blades, knives and forks from a cab. He swallows pounds of tissue paper. Every one is happy, even the very clothy peasantry who stick out of their heavy embroidered coats and breeches uncomfortably like jagged chunks of red and blue rock, and every bit of them itching. A man who sells a razor and two blades for two reales, talks like a clown, swallows paper, makes fun of the old stork on the tower, is a wonder. He says:

' The people who buy these earrings will not pay ten pesetas, nor nine, nor eight, nor seven, nor six, nor five, nor four, nor three, nor two, nor one, nor the three reales. For two reales and no more I will give them, on one condition. That she who is not satisfied and says I have deceived her shall bring them back to me the next time I am here.'

How does he do it ? It is a mystery. What happens to the paper he swallows ? It is a mystery—for you can be sure he never swallows the paper. It appears life is a mystery.

Then the crowd is scattered by the tinkle of a bell. Off come the men's hats. There is one man who will buy no more earrings for any one. A deal coffin is borne on six shoulders across the Plaza between a file of raw men holding candles. The priests are white and black and gold. They advance the high silver crucifix. The priests are singing—not the song of the women, the song of the water, the living waters, but the dirge song of the earth, of the dust taking back its own box by box. The priests' Latin snores under the narrow windowed houses. No voices are more of the earth than men's voices. Voices leaden as wine and as dull and maddening. The sadness of the monotonous voices of men is intolerable and heart-breaking. The young men shall utterly fail. Is there any more terrifying sight than a procession of men?

There are no women in the procession. They appear at the balconies. The mysteries are no things for women in this men's country. The procession stops under the arch of the city gates. The crowd is black in the pit of the hill. The coffin is placed on a trestle and the mourners file by while the bearers rest. The priests, grave in black, white, and gold, return alone, unfollowed with their crucifix, symbols off duty.

Up to the shoulders. Under the archway the coffin is mounted to the shoulders of the bearers. 'Hup.' The bearers march, the mourners march, the priestless crowd moves on, the stragglers return. The coffin is borne out of the town into the country at a rapid stride anxiously, as though what is borne must not be borne too long. The crowd almost runs over the iron bridge, to the left it descends by the altar-cloth of evening poplars, now like candles that have gone out, and in the smoke of white dust advances over a mile of treeless, wilderness road to a small cemetery of cypresses black as priests, white tombs tipped with the sun's gold—a compact cemetery like a fort within one white wall, black, white, and gold like a priest's vestment. To this the crowd almost flies, diminishing till it is a great ragged crow sweeping down and bearing something away.

THE WEDDING

The green night is scissored away from the roofs, and bats circle low to the iron balconies of houses white as thick moons. The windows are yellow rectangles of light. Below in the street, crowds of women are standing on the doorsteps, eyes glittering with joyful expectancy. A hundred barbers in the middle of shaving their victims, who lie back with raw skulls as comic as cannibals with a tattoo pattern of lather, leave them, run to stand at the door, with the harness makers, the watch repairers, the cobblers, the strap makers, the straw mat makers, the tobacconists, the oil merchants ; and all are joking and talking. Death is a social duty ; but a wedding is a splendid defiance of society that puts new heart into people who have forgotten what it is to do a thing because they want to do it. Strange, happy emotions move slowly like smoke in every one.

' Santiago,' cries the cheap Jack looking at his scattering crowd and packing up. ' What's the matter ? What passes ? Ah, a wedding. Ah, ah, they won't want me for to-night then. They won't want any of us to-night, eh ? To-night,' he cries, putting his hand to his lips and blowing a kiss which he watches rapturously as it floats up like a bird, ' none of us will be wanted.'

The group of soldiers buckle their faces into bent

hoops of yellow laughter. Uh, ha, ha ! Uh, ha, ha !
And as is the Spanish custom, they sware by their
private parts.

The little soldiers in blue coats and red hats and
khaki breeches straddle over to the street corner.
Amid cries broad and thin, cries like bells, comes the
wedding crowd. It is not a procession. It is an
onrush. The bride and bridegroom walk the street
arm in arm, followed by a cheering body of people.
' Long live the bride ! ' shout the relatives, wine-red
with shouting. ' Viva ! ' the reply.

He is a young man, thin and shining. A shiny coat,
and shiny trousers, a shiny face, shiny hair. She is a
young widow of a certain amplitude, of well charged
bosom with a cup custard chin. A comb rides high
in her hair, and from it hangs the peaked mantilla of
dry black lace. As he is shiny, obvious, she is dry,
dull, mysterious as lace, a woman who, sitting in a
small white Spanish room on a weighty chair carved
with exquisite cruelty, would drain up the air by her
presence. She is a shopkeeper's widow, and is lucky
to be married again ; and to this young man whose
coat is a little too long for him, a thin, exhausted
young man with a veneer of vitality in his eyes and
his gesticulations. In the sun-rotted provinces where
the streets smell of wine and oil and perspiration as
though the houses were wearing warm white shifts
that have never been washed, the men of the towns
are aged and spent at thirty ; but the women are
stout, rich as hives, deep with somnolent, teeming
life.

But the wedding ! Long live the bride ! The street

is shouting. The wedding party hurries into the
fonda, where at long tables scores of guests are to
take their seats. There is a pile of plates before
every one, thick plates and black wine bottles. The
oil and the fat and the sauces that wine will wash
down! There is a sibilation of soup. The shutters
are drawn so that the vulgar crowd cannot see
the pomp of the wedding feast. But they can
hear it.

'Viva the bride!' 'Viva!'
'Viva the bridegroom!' 'Viva!'
'Viva the mother of the bride!' 'Viva!'
'Viva the father of the bride!' 'Viva!'
'Viva the mother of the bridegroom!' 'Viva!'
'Viva the father of the bridegroom!' 'Viva!'
'Viva the brother of the bride!' 'Viva!'

Viva every one and everything. Viva the soup, the
olive oil, the garlic, the olives, the wine. Above all,
viva the garlic and the oil. One is baptised in water
but married in oil.

The feast continues late, the streets empty. The
town is silent except in the Plaza, where late soldiers
and priests and men are explaining to one another at
great length why they did this in that particular way,
the endless self-justification of the all-enveloping
Spanish ego. Monologues, for no Spaniard ever
listens. How much more interesting, even fantastic,
is his 'yo' than this curious boring 'Yo' who is
speaking. The town is silent except in that fonda
where the banquet roars and boils, thunders, crackles
like a furnace, and the slants of light beam through
the cracks of the shutters as though through furnace

doors. Long live the bride, long live the father of the bride. . . .

The party retires to the garden at the back of the fonda to dance. An electric piano begins to throb, munch notes, weep, and squeeze out music. Round and round gaudy notes, yellow notes, skipping out and thumping and heeling the serious tango. The bride and bridegroom dance together. The guests dance. No one else is allowed to dance with the bride. One hears the slow scratching of feet over the dusty ground and the lean dust rises like a vapour. The dancers scrape up and down in weird figures, turn round, arrive slowly again, stepping sideways and starting back, pausing a step or two to loosen a collar, pull up a sock, wipe a forehead, reach a button. They dance under acacias where the dust is sweet and the stars like bunches of blossom rise and fall with the shoulders of the dancers. The shadows cross one another in a duel of rapiers passing from body to body, piercing all harmlessly ; couples slip out of shadow into light, are stabbed by it and slip again into shadow. Electric lights shine in the garden, electric green night, electric notes tumbling in great bunching, squeezing, hurrying torrents of music, kilowatts of passion and love. The piano stands alone like a wide black mouth bubbling, drinking, blowing, sucking an enormous plate of soup, trying to swallow chiming, dripping strings of vermicelli, and thumping a table for more at every gulp. Thump, thump, thumper, hit, thumper, thumper hit thumper—vowing three tragic kingdoms to her beautiful eyes, treading with her the tops of moon-

filled mountains alone, while the world becomes less
than the shadows of rapiers trembling over a river
of music. . . .

The sereno or night watchman is standing in the
shadow of the cathedral. He is an old man carrying a
lamp, a steel javelin, a belt of enormous keys round
his waist, and he walks up and down with a cigarette
in his mouth. There are three clashes of arms in the
belfry. Three o'clock. He puts his hand to his cheek
and bawls, fearful of blasting his teeth out, ' Ave
Maria Purissima, three o'clock and a fine night.'

The words fall like a crash of rods in the street, a
sneeze of iron. Mongrels howl in all the parishes
where late bells bang. He listens. He looks up the
street, cobbled between the moon walls, emptily
passing out of the town, over the bridge into the
nothing of night. The music has ceased and the
people have left the fonda. The feast had passed like
a bright wind. He draws his cigarette into a point
of red. In no window of the town is there a light.

CHAPTER XIV.
NOTHING

I had now marched 105 miles from Badajoz, and at a low pass of the Gredos I turned my back on Extremadura and crossed into the province of Salamanca. I cut the journey in two at a long stringy village called Aldea Nueva del Camino, a point at which the remains of the old Roman road can be seen. After twenty miles of wilderness closing into ravines and opening into meadows and hills down which the long-horned cows came charging, with bells clanging, in terrifying manner across the road, I saw kneeling distantly at the rites of solitude the cerulean assembly of the Hurdes ; and as, conquering, I approached, the acclaiming Goat mountains and the Sierra de Béjar rising to their feet before me.

I sat dosing under a tree waiting for the tense power of the heat to wane, in a stupor of cattle bells, when I saw an old man walking towards me. He greeted me, ' Good-day. The companion is resting ? ' He was tall and stooped slightly, a man of noble stature and with a beauty and gravity in his long striding motions. His hair was grey, his eyes had the changeless blue of the sky in a dark ochre skin. His face was thin, his teeth white and full and perfect, giving a scholarly gentleness and, with the steady inquiry of his eyes, a judge-like shrewdness to his speech. He carried a horn on his back and wore leather aprons fancifully tooled, to his trouser legs. He told me he was minding the cattle for his master.

He sat down under the tree beside me. ' Friend,' he said, ' seeing you here alone, I thought to myself, that is not a man from these lands but a stranger. I will go and see who it is. I will go and see who it is for it cannot be a man of these lands, I thought to myself. So I came up thinking, I will see who it is, and there as you tell me, friend, you are a stranger and not a man of these lands. Didn't I think so ? ' He chuckled at his sagacity. He asked me the usual questions discreetly. ' Man, I am glad you are well, and that your family is well, and that your wife is well, and that times are not ill with you,' he said with the curled lip of the kindly pedant. ' I am glad I came over to see who you might be, for I thought you must be alone and a stranger. O man, I regret, I apologise—I did not offer you any tobacco,' he handed me his leather pouch—' Man, I apologise, I do not know—being alone one forgets one's manners.'

I liked the fashion of his ' Man.' The word united us with the spark of nobility. I was man and he was man. We were two noble beings confronted on a field of cloth of gold. And the word as he spoke it warmed the limbs like wine. Spain is a country of men as France is a woman's country. ' Man,' say the men to each other, the children to each other, and even women to women. Hombre—the word has the authority of a prophet, the power of an oath, the richness of crumpling thunder. The sound of the word on Spanish lips tightens mind and body with

awe. Who can forget the beating of his heart when
he first heard the opening peal of Unamuno's 'Del
Sentimiento Tragico de la Vida':

'Ni lo humano ni la humanidad, ni el adjetivo
simple, ni el adjetivo sustantivado, sino el sustantivo
concreto ; el hombre. El hombre de carne y hueso,
el que nace, sufre y muere—sobre todo muere—el
que come y bebe y juega y duerme y piensa y quiere,
el hombre que se ve y quien se oye, el hermano, el
verdadero hermano.'

So ; 'Man,' exclaimed he who was seated beside
me. 'You are right to rest in the heat. In the heat
one is right to rest. One should rest. The lack of
rain is bad. If God does not want to send the rain
though, you may complain above, below, everywhere, but that won't make the rain come.' His lips
smiled ironically as he thought of the impossibility
of satisfying the transparent vanity of his Castilian
God when it came to the question of rain.

He dug his stick into the ground and began rolling
his cigarette. He looked up at the wide based
heavens. The sun had grooved his face and fined it
down to the spare traits of nobility.

'Well, man,' he cried out resonantly with joy.

'What do you think of this life ?' I asked.

'Ha, ha,' he laughed, the embroidered laughter of a
faun, and by that laughter awakened all the pagan
gold and light from their repose in his countenance,
stirred immemorial associations with the sun adoring
earth. 'Ha, ha ! What do I think of this life ? Of this
life ? Well, what should I think of it ?' He paused
and shrugged his shoulders smiling, 'Nothing.'

' Nothing ? ' I echoed.

' Nothing ! Nothing, nothing, nothing. When it is good, good. When it is bad, good too, for who can change it ? One remains living until—well, at last one is put into the ground,' said he, shooting out a spurt of earth with his stick and watching it fall.

He went on enjoying his good humour. ' When one eats well, good. When one eats ill, good. Then —nothing.'

' Nothing ? ' I echoed.

' Nothing, nothing, man,' he said. With one poke of his stick he had reduced the anxiety of the world to this.

Twenty head of cattle came stampeding through the trees with bells gone mad.

' Bueyes ! Vaca-a-a-a ! ' shouted he, jumping up, watching them lolloping and arching around the wide pasture with the calves skipping and bucking before them, large eyes innocent of the heavy gaiety of those old beasts, their parents.

' Man ! ' he said, ' I am glad I came over. Glad. Man, I said to myself, there is a stranger to these lands. I shall go and see who the friend is. He is sitting there alone. And thus we have spoken together. My regards to your family and to your wife, and a good journey. Vaya usted con Dios.'

I continued my journey towards Aldea Nueva, wondering how I should be received there ; whether I should have to sleep on a sack on the floor of some posada stable ; and feeling as I sighted the village, scattered like a heap of red stones in a pit of water-pouring hills, the momentary thrill of fear that gives pause to travellers as they approach a strange destination.

On the outskirts of the village, where the rising ground was becoming fertile, precious water was being carried by banked irrigation channels from a shallow river into the ravines. Men were stripping cork bark from the trees, driving dust clouds of sheep, herding goats. The village was a higgledy-piggledy of streets, and the houses had long wooden balconies hanging like broken bird-cages from the walls. The village square was a piece of open ground in a heap of boulders, and the houses were thrown pell-mell into the tree tops above it. A fountain was spurting forth four lashing arcs of water. The evening sun glittered like the lace of a mantilla.

I met a man who had wandered all over Extremadura, and had even crossed the frontier into Portugal and so to Lisbon, on a donkey, buying skins and selling them to a tanner in Salamanca, seventy miles away.

'For twenty-five years I have been travelling all over the Castiles and the south buying skins.'

I had scarcely sat down in the café of the fonda and made known my wants before a young man, starved anxiousness in his eyes, who was evidently a kind of waiter at the beck and call of every one, including the very pretty daughter of the innkeeper, came and talked with me. He came sniffling up like a scared Spanish dog, waggling, cringing, hoping, daring, whining. We talked about my journey. He was determined to get in my good books, until some one more interesting to imitate and follow about came to him. For every time I raised my arm for a gesture, he raised his. If I sighed, he sighed. If I stamped my foot and complained how slow the people in the fonda were, he stamped his foot and said it was indeed an atrocity. In a moment he was copying all my facial expressions. I put my elbows on the table and on came his immediately, edging their way across till our four arms were on the point of meeting. Then he began to hiss desperate confidences to me. ' Do you know the most important things in life ? ' he asked. ' These.'

He pointed to his mouth and his clothes. ' Eating and clothing. The rest, nothing.' He whispered eagerly, and looking round as though he were being eavesdropped or pursued.

At this there was a crash of broken glass and a stone dropped under our table. We started up to see a mob of village children throwing stones at the fonda. Angrily out of a trap door in the floor and startlingly close to us, popped the proprietor of the inn. He was an excited and earnest little fellow with his shirt unbuttoned and his indignant breast bared, as it were, for the executioner's knife. He was the kind of innkeeper who would have sheltered William Tell, and in those days would surely have been shot by the Austrians, if only because his noble and inn-keeperly breast seemed to invite a fusilade of martyrising bullets. He rushed to the door, cursing the young man who, seizing a napkin, began a wild pretence of driving off an invisible enemy by snapping it everywhere in the air. The shouting and stones increased ; but when the proprietor appeared

at the door the children fled screaming. He came
back and, after abusing the young waiter, dropped
into his trap door again. The waiter went up and
stood in the doorway with his chest indignant,
bulging, snapping his napkin. He returned to me.
' Those children, I drove them off,' he said.

The cause of this joyfulness was soon made clear.
A travelling company of Aragonese dancers was
dressing in weird costumes behind the inn, and was
being reminded of its promise to drive round the
neighbouring hamlets. Greatly protesting, the company appeared in shabby and vivid mantones de
Manila, the men in knee breeches, blue stockings,
and open shirts. The men got into one car, and the
women, with their babies, which looked as though
they might have been born on the tour, into another,
and after a preliminary twanging and chorus of singing and guitars, they drove off over the rocks, the
spanking cars bucking like ponies and half the village
cheering after them.

The village and the café now emptied. The young
waiter slippered over to me and sat down at my
table again, but before he had time to put his elbows
on the table, the pretty daughter of the innkeeper, a
Murillo Virgin, came out with a tray of glasses and
called him to put them away. A squall of irritation
passed over his face. When will there be peace?
Coming. Is there no peace in this life? Called here,
pulled there, coming.

He put three glasses away, and seeing her go out of
the door with water-jars, knew she would stand an
hour at that fountain talking to the other girls who

would be coming with their water-jars too. So he left the rest of the glasses and came wagging his tail, slinking up to me. ' Iay,' he sighed. ' Those travelling companies eat money. They make money and eat like the rich. That is how I would like to live, to live and eat like the rich. And you are going to Béjar ? Well, friend, I came from Béjar yesterday. Oh, yes, I am new here. I walked from Béjar yesterday. Came on foot. It was horrible.'

The swipe of the four-tailed water dragon outside, and the yellow road curled like a hot monster over the mountains into red Béjar standing on that hump called the Cuerpo del Hombre—the body of a man. When I was in Plasencia he was grinding, grinding over the low long pass from Béjar. He continued : ' I had four pesetas. I came searching for a living. You also, perhaps, come searching for a living. I heard there was a job on the road, and I walked ten miles to it, but the foreman was a brute, the hours were too long—I do not like long hours—and the wages not as high as they ought to be. I prefer nothing to anything that is too small. I came on not knowing what to do. For two days I have this job, while these touring people are here. Two days and then nothing more. It is an atrocity. I am called here, there, everywhere. There is no peace. With money one can have peace. I don't know what I'm going to do. I did not tell my mother I was coming. She was against me. She would drive me into slavery. She hates my fiancée. I did not even tell my fiancée I was going. Perhaps,' he said, dog's eyes startled at the thought, ' I ought to let her know.

Yes, she must know. Do you not think it is better?'

He jumped up happily. He was greatly relieved, and then he became glum. 'How can I let her know? I cannot write.' I offered to write the letter for him. I took a scratchy pen and paper. How should I begin this letter to his lady? I put the delicate question tactfully. A look of fright came over his face. 'I do not know,' he said. 'I have never written a letter. How would you?'

'Well—— ' I began.

'I don't know,' he said. 'It is difficult. Do you think, Muy señora mia, Dear Madam, would be all right?'

So I began; Dear Madam, I regret I find myself obliged not to take the situation on the road, for it was nine hours and only seven pesetas. Tell my mother I regret she thinks I am undutiful, but 'quien no sale no vale,' he who stays at home is worth nothing. Tell your mother I will be rich. Tell my mother I am contrite. Tell my mother to send a change of shirts. Tell your mother I am here and have my bed and my food. Tell my mother I am happy. Tell my mother to send my clean shirts for Sunday by the diligence, and come yourself by Thursday and we shall go to Madrid. I have ten pesetas.

'And how shall I end it?' I asked.

'I will print my name,' he said. 'I can write my Christian name. Fernando. Ya! like this. F-E-N-A-D-O.'

The café was still empty. A waste of marble-topped tables with a dirty floor, stained with cigarette-ends and spittle, and with an irritating damp and dusty smell.

'Yes,' he said, snuffling his face with its large wet doggy eyes towards me and lolling his tongue out 'I shall go to Madrid. We shall both go. There is a train. There is a station a mile from here. We shall get married in Madrid, and I will get a job. I have always wanted my mother to go to Madrid and be a caretaker. But she is obstinate. There is nothing more obstinate in the world than a woman. How shall we go to Madrid without money? Oh, that's easy. Travel under the seat. Many people ride under the seat. Choose a compartment full of stout women, their dresses and petticoats cover up everything. It is safe. It is safe as long as people are good and honourable. But when people are evil and deceitful they give you away. That is the difficulty. There are so many evil people in the world to prevent you from eating, who want all the food and money. Béjar is a town of evil people. Those who have plenty are always the worst.'

The young sloppy spaniel curled about the place. The pretty girl came in with splashing water-jars and abused him in hoity-toity voice about the glasses; but he smiled and licked his lips and leaned against the counter, and put on his face such an air of mock contrition that she laughed as gaily as spinning water, and he laughed too, big woofs of laughter, and began a great flirtation. He would be sorry to leave in two days. Why would he be sorry to leave? For every one was so kind to him. That is, the others chased him about, called him here, there, above, below, and everywhere, but she didn't. She understood him. Oh, no. Ai yai. Her eyes were as light as larks, and dark as pansies. Her eyes were like two larks singing or black water beating into silver at the fountain. It was such luck the dancers were here. He loved dancing, didn't she ? He would give his life to be dancing, passing life without care. . . .

At this the earth opened ; out of the trap door rose the girl's father, bosom still bared for execution, and calling loudly for the young man. Coming ! no peace ! What a man wants is peace. To be a rich man and have peace. Coming. Stepping from table to table he went with a pretence of doing a great deal, slashing each table with a napkin as he went. Three peasants were sitting at a table. Three coffees. Ha, ha ! three coffees. He stood there looking at them, smiling at them, listening to what they had to say, following every word of it, unconsciously imitating their expressions and gestures and their laughter. He was wealthy. He was sitting down with three men ordering three coffees from a little misery of a waiter, and he was talking about a load of cork bark. Dios mio ! if that was all they were going to offer him they could keep it. It wouldn't pay to transport it. No, it wouldn't, of course it wouldn't. Not at that price ! *What?* At *that* price ? No ! No ! Ha, ha ! he was rich and could eat. How he could eat !

  ' Here you, boy, what about those coffees, standing there staring like an animal ? ' He jumped out of his dreams. O my God, coming, coming. . . .

The master chased him about from table to table as
you chase a fly. Here, they want beer. Or coffee
there. In came a tall handsome man wearing a wide
black hat, not a villager. Oh no, he was one of the
rich, a commercial traveller. He came in with two
guardias in green and yellow. The little waiter ran
up to them smiling, laughing. He looked up into
their faces, walking backwards down the room.
They took no notice of him. He seemed to beg.
Unknown to them he joined them. He stood listening, smiling, darkening. When they scowled, he
scowled. When they laughed, he laughed ; and when
they boasted, he threw out his chest and measured
his stride among the tables by theirs. The master
called him, but he was lost. He was a commercial
traveller. He was tall, wore a cloak like that with a
crimson lining, a collar, a hat like that. He took
trains. Somebody paid that he might take trains.
He sold things. Hundreds of things. To-day he was
in the Aldea, to-morrow in Béjar, then in Salamanca,
the capital ; paid well, travelling, above all eating
well. Up and down he followed them eagerly looking up into their faces. His napkin dropped from
his hand. . . .

I slept in a clean, uncurtained, but newly whitewashed alcove. The Aragonese came in at four in the
morning, and getting into their own alcoves we
snored in unison until seven o'clock. I woke to see
the sun's beams thrust into the fonda like the golden
arms of one searching out sheaves and grasping them.
Sitting up in bed I observed that through the night
the pictures of two watery nineteenth century

generals, with that meek insipidity of countenance which the wearing of whiskers gave them, had also been my companions. Their sad oil-cloth eyes watched me pack my haversack and depart from the shade of their dead and shiny whiskers for ever.

I went down into the café, but it was scarcely possible to see across the room for dust. The chairs were piled in squads on the tables, and among them, slipper heels snapping at the boards, went the little waiter. I asked him what about some breakfast. ' I don't know,' he said, his mouth dropping open. Then the pretty girl came in with a handful of charcoal and, soaking a rag in olive oil, set fire to it, and put rag and charcoal into a hole in the stone counter underneath an urn. Immediately he was with her talking, laughing, hee-hawing like a young ass, this, this, and this-ing, leaning against the counter with his napkin falling over his shoulder. Stupid spaniel chin, hungry spaniel eyes.

That day I ascended by hills bursting with water and carolling with it from a hundred throats and streams. The fields fell white and yellow with buttercups and daisies, the hedgerows poured into cascades of lilac, hawthorn, and wild roses. The road was carved in broad flinty bastions and terraces cork-screwing up the pass, but I left it and climbed across country up the face of the mountain. At the top I had arrived at another climate. The trees were still bare, and but faintly misted in green as though they had not yet drunken spring's winds and rains of wine, though the southern plains had long been green.

The clearing was pencilled with wide open beech and sycamore where the skies shuttered up like opening windows from the boles of the trees, and the firm northerly winds sailed through high as returning swallows.

CHAPTER XV

SUN OF FIRE

As I stood in that break of the Gredos at the boundary stone, with Castile a thousand feet below, the whole limitless prospect flowing into the blue cyclone forms of the Hurdes swept up against Portugal, the dumbness of the scene brought back to my mind an encounter with a Basque woman I had had many years before. Not in the Gredos, but hundreds of miles eastward, in the Guadarramas. These are the eastern wing of the Gredos system, and as I paused a few moments, I felt passing along Spain's spine the shock and message of a memory, the memory of silence.

She was pretty. She was fair. Her eyes were blue as the sight of northern sea. A face that was still round and childish was being grained and worked by the mountain sun. She was even buxom. Her age might have been thirty-five and she was as simple as a dumpling. She ran lightly about with the innocent gravity of a calf, a brown, big-eyed calf ; pouted, teased, flirted, and laughed her own language to herself like a bird, or pausing puckered her brows and tried to say something that would not come, in Castilian. Ending always with a pretty childlike desolation :

' I—Basque. Not speak well. My husband— Castilian.'

She came from the Basque provinces and he from

Valladolid in Old Castile. She could not speak or
understand much of his language ; and he could not
speak or understand any of hers ; nothing more than
' Kiss me,' or ' I love you,' or ' Do you love me,'
' Yes,' or ' No.'

They lived in a little stone lodge on a high burned
spur of the Guadarrama ; and she had once tried to
tell me he was ' mecanico ' and went down into the
plains for days at a stretch while she remained above
alone, seeing no one except shepherds, taciturn and
aged as rock, or men driving the long horned bulls
into Cercedilla, or gypsies dark as summer, crossing
the pass from one province to another.

The lodge was in the highest silences of the Guadarrama, in winter remote in snow, in summer under
a sun of fire. I climbed one June in that barren range,
which is built from four to nine thousand feet above
the sea and divides the arid tablelands of the two
Castiles. The blades of the Seven Peaks, scarred and
bent in the silent opposings of wind and sun and cold,
are drawn out naked as metal from their deep scab-
bards of pine and bite the sky. At these heights the
rock appears to breathe a flame. There is the acrid
tang of wild lavender and the heat of the resinous
firs. There is neither wind nor sound, and the tops of
the passes seem to be the wide thresholds of the
ultimate solitude.

About half a mile from the top of one of these
passes was her stone lodge just on the road. I knew
I could get something to eat there, perhaps a
pair of eggs, as the Castilians say, fried in olive
oil till the yoke is crisp and green ; or some

ancient sausage seasoned with garlic, gnarled as timber.

There was a bare room with two tables, three benches, and a stick fire burning on the hearth, and on a pole over the fire were dangled at least two score sausages curled like short and stout little grubs.

'Under this sun of fire,' said the woman looking at me, moving a step back, puzzled prettily. Then,

'You—here in the winter? I have seen you, no? Yes. You were—how you say?—O Virgin, I still —not speak the Castellano. I—Basque.'

She was right : it was not my first visit. Two winters before I had stopped for a meal at this lodge on the brow of the world's top, when the snow like a white door had shut out the plains below. Two years had passed and she had lived there almost wordlessly, silent within a silence.

She had two children and some goats and chickens. To these she gurgled strange complaining sounds in the Basque tongue, and talked to herself as she busied about the room. No one could understand her ; she was unknowable, like a tree or like one of the Seven Peaks.

It was so rarely any one stopped at her house that she stood watching me with pride. She pitied me for my climb. She fussed over me, bringing an unusual number of knives and forks, and a clean napkin for me. But on her lips, all the time, were words she could not fashion into speech. She scolded.

'Before, you—you—have a wife ! ! ' An accusing dainty light of fear in her eyes. She added something harsh in Basque.

' She has gone away to her country,' I said.

' Away ? ' Her voice emptied its sound like a bell.
' A little, pretty one. A —. Then you quarrel ? '

' No,' I said. ' She has gone to her country.'

She became quickly sad and shook her head, unable
to understand something.

' Country,' she murmured. ' My husband and I—
No ! No ! No ! '

And ran to the door looking over the deep ravines
of pines and over the knobs of the lower spurs lying
like a far blue seacoast at her feet.

She returned to the fire and made me some coffee,
singing in Basque to herself, at times speaking aloud.
She brought me some slices of sausage. She fried me
a dish of eggs in olive oil; and as I ate them she
watched me wistfully with head nodded to one side
and then to the other, gathering words and on the
point of speaking them, as a dog with eyes sad with
language will try and speak to a man. She began to
tap her feet and give quick shallow sighs, her cheeks
flushed and a fluent blaze came into her blue eyes. A
few words loosened, and she could restrain herself
no longer. She blurted at last,

' My husband and I—we quarrel. It is a terrible
thing.'

She watched me like a naughty child to see how I
took the news ; then came in a ringing child voice a
stumbling cascade of confession. She must make
some one understand.

' Ah, yes. We quarrel. We—it is necessary but few
words to quarrel. It is the Ford. Ah, yes. It is bad. It is,
how do you say ? second-hand. Constantly it breaks.

It spends money. It is the ruin. And three days he is away, my husband. It is so bad he takes it to Madrid. How it costs. Always he is away; it is the Ford. It is a waste, and for three days a week, too, it leaves me alone. I don't know—it is a terrible thing. Ah, yes. We quarrel. We quarrel, with our heads, no?'

'With your minds,' I suggested.

'Who knows,' she said, not understanding.

So they opposed like two goats head to head, mind to mind, locked silently month after month in the silence below the pass; after the winter the thaw singing in the earth, twinkling on the brief mountain turf, whistling, moving, gurgling, and speaking among the rocks, the scrub and the lavender, and spouting trilling pipes of water from the snow boughs of the firs. Barky pools swelled and blackened in the woods. The earth was alive with wet. The hard pelts of the Guadarrama balds were brightened with daisies white as young clouds, and with tinkling daffodils. You could feel on the new air the young precious breathing of the straight pines. The looping road shone and loosened in the wet and the sun. Till again the blue air deepened to high summer and over the splendid crowns of the tree tops passed the brief shadows of the hawks. Hundreds of emerald lizards rippled under the stones like water; below the villages on the floor of New Castile— Guadarrama, Cercedilla, and Escorial—places of men and speech. Alone, bared from the scabbard, the silent Seven Peaks under the sun of fire.

CHAPTER XVI

MEN OF PEACE

Béjar is a town of one street almost a mile long flagged between tall and overhanging houses, and as you walk through the place you see the snow mountains, lean and sculptured above the house-tops, like the still and impending clouds of Castile.

The roosting owl houses of Béjar are built against the extreme cold of winter—Nueve meses de invierno y très de infierno, they say : Nine months of winter and three of hell—when even Extremadura can be covered with snow and the passes are closed. Each house has its miradores or enclosed glass balconies fixed to the walls like crazy boxes, the western ones throwing out the fires of sunset like the nostrils of a dragon. No dragon clung so desperately as Béjar, with the red claws of its side streets tearing into the flanks of that strange ridge, Cuerpo del Hombre, body of a man. The dragon's nostrils are taxed too, for I found a notice on the wall of a café, and in the Mayor's own lean and scratchy hand, requiring all citizens liable to pay the tax on their miradores to appear at the market, signed with great circumstance, flourish, and a shower of authoritative blots by the Mayor, Don Fructuoso Jesus Gonzalez. Fruitful Jesus !

The chief occupation of Béjar is the making of slippers. In nearly every booth is a cobbler. Sixes and sevens of cobblers squat on the floor with boards on their knees winding the rope soles of the canvas slippers about nails stuck in the board. In Béjar, where every one has white slippers, they are made with bright flowers and butterflies stamped on the toes.

The ayuntamiento, where Don Fructuoso rules, is yellow and ripe as a camembert, and before it the Plaza ripples a flagged lake of stones. Here the jar sellers lay out their wares in the road like skittles to be knocked down, or like some queer Egyptian game dug out of a tomb ; and stout bakers in rough and itchy clothes push wheelbarrows of bread, loaves heavy and large enough to brain a man. At night the stars print a mystic halo about the silver head of Candelario, where the Virgin of the town dwells, and Don Fructuoso and his taxpayers lie below snoring or silent. Only the northern wind pitters on the glass and Salamanca mules kick in their stables. Ave Maria Purissima, four o'clock and a fine night.

Béjar is a disheartening place to leave, for one has to climb, I should guess, a thousand feet out of it in laborious miles curving up to the back of those three humps of rock that stand like a dromedary above the town. The land becomes dreary and withered, skimped and starved pasture. I remember now the awe I felt as looking back on the climb I saw the Candelario, that below had appeared gentle and delicate as the Virgin, had now risen to a terrifying proportion, standing up in the stirrups of its streams and overpowering like some gigantic rider who might any moment take it into his head to ride me down. Even now he leaned towards me. . . .

The sky became as hard as stone, the air torrid, thin, poor, and barren, the earth was shrunken like the face of a dying man. This was Salamanca, the central tableland of Spain that is hollow eyed with drought, withered by cold, crumbled by heat, with its rivers dried up and its few trees lilac skeletons among boulders that are a field of skulls. Sky shrill as a starved man's eyes. It was like climbing over the ruins of a graveyard.

Poor people, struggling people, hammered down like coffin nails into this unprofitable land, were driving their few sheep into Béjar for the market, or came in dozens on donkeys and mules, bulging, wagging, shaking, shouting among themselves in strange jerking cavalcades. All fell silent as they passed me, people pale as the earth, with their belongings heaped in panniers and the white dust smoking among them as they shouted. Only one spoke to me, and that was near the top of this six mile agony, before the full desolation of the province had come before my eyes. He was a jolly-eyed man in black breeches and a wide, low-crowned hat—a costume that is getting rare now—and seeing me come, he stopped his donkey and called out, 'Hail, the companion. So we are reduced to beggary that we have to go on foot. Bueno hombre. Good journey, man, and walk with God,' he bawled, with a great stress on the God. A hearty, solid, red-faced, a strong and omnipotent God, a man like himself was the God of the man on that donkey. A God like a mountain, or like a wind longer than a rich man's pocket, a monstrous shout,

a shrewd and mighty joker. A God who might walk
and pretend to be a beggar. The kind of God you
would need to walk with in a country like this. I
was up to that pass and scrambling down the face of
it on the other side in no time, with an eye for
where I should find the road again, curled like a
whip.

Poor country, poor inns. Fifteen miles before I
could hope to find anything. I passed through two
villages, ruinous places falling to pieces, with broken
balconies, shored-up walls, windowless houses, as
red as a brickyard. The walls of the cottages from
now onward fifty miles to Salamanca were covered
with large red tiles with vertical stripes of mortar
between them as though every place were wearing a
football jersey. These villages were always deserted
but for a few dogs, who rushed out at me furiously
barking and ran away with their tails between their
legs. The Candelario had now risen and lengthened
until, on rising ground, I saw a vast range rise up
like a white choir as far as the eye could see, the
hot and ochreous Gredos in ethereal procession,
snow peaks like candles with bending flame borne
eastward.

An old peasant woman in a green embroidered
dress and shawl was standing by the side of the road
with a bit of rope in her hand. She had a crafty,
knowing face, and eyes jingling like carefully
counted small change. She cackled, ' Good-day, sir,
and have you seen my black donkey, my donkey
that is black, as you passed ? '

There was an old man ploughing a patch of stone

with a yoke of cows : ' Gee up, butterfly,' he
shouted to his cows, and when he heard the woman's
question, he roared with laughter and tapped his
forehead significantly with his finger, ' *Her* black
donkey ! ' he cried, ' her black donkey ! Ha, ha ! '
She had no black donkey.

After Guijuelo, small brick-red town with a railway
pinned on to it by a thread of telegraph wire that
had been stitched across the land, the country began
to roll and become more fertile. The leagues rose
and fell, red ploughed soil without a crop appearing
yet. Beside me marched the juggling, crooked, bony
telegraph poles strung together by their wires, ridiculous, cadging, eyeless, one-legged companions
humming between their four white teeth like idiots.
How many thousand of them to Salamanca ? Sapless
poles stuck in the road, never fed, and no one but a
woodpecker to care what becomes of them. They
rose and fell with the rhythmic undulations of the
leagues.

I passed the night at the village of La Maya,
twenty-seven miles from Béjar and twenty from
Salamanca. It was a small red village scarcely visible
among the combed furrows, a heap of stones with
a bit of church tower sticking out of it like a
spade handle. On the tableland the villages are
far apart, and between Salamanca and Béjar there
were no towns within sixty miles and only seven
tiny ruinous hamlets, which appeared to have
been shattered by the resounding sword blow of
the road.

La Maya was a place of low granite cottages. The

village was empty, and only in the evening appeared human forms, women in black passing noiselessly as Arabs, with water-jars on their heads, going to the fountain.

Three noisy commercial travellers from Salamanca spent a few hours in the village, having brought their cloth on donkeys from the station two miles away. Failing to sell their cloth to the canny peasantry, who preferred to go into Salamanca on market day and buy their own, the travellers sat down in the Parador and drank brandy, carrying on a lewd conversation for the benefit of the innkeeper's daughter. She was a heavy creature who carried a baby at the breast and regarded the travellers sullenly as a beast, hating every one. She was thick necked and with a low forehead, and stood with legs apart and head lowered as though about to charge her enemies and gore them. One of the travellers, a man with the waist of a wasp, was an Andalusian from Huelva. He drivelled away like the little Andalusian señorito he was, but neither the innkeeper nor his daughter could see anything funny about him. The innkeeper drew at his cigarette, watching everything rapidly with knife-tipped eyes, and spoke, disregarding the Andalusian, slowly and carefully in the Salamantina drawl to me, 'Va usted a Salamanca-a-a-a, mañana-a-a-a por la mañana-a-a-a.'

The Andalusian buzzed up to me with an offensive ingratiation, and said, 'Cardee, Leerpool, Engleesh, plenty monee. O yes, spik Englee.'

Which was to indicate he had spent two years in the mines at Cardiff.

There was an excitable young man with them, too. He drank more brandy than all. He chucked the woman under the chin, but she snatched up his money and growled at him like some resenting dog. Rebuffed, he came up and offered to exchange coats with me. He said his was worth twenty-five duros (about £4, 10s.) and was the best coat in the world, and the only reason that he wanted to change it was because he was my friend. I had become exasperated by these vulgar creatures, so angrily I shouted back that mine was worth a hundred duros, that nothing on earth would ever persuade me to sell or exchange it, and that he could go to the devil. 'Nothing, nothing, nothing,' I cried, and, finally, 'nothing.'

That drove the young man off to the counter, and after he had picked up my haversack and stroked my coat and fiddled with my hat, he stared at the woman and she glowered back. He drank more brandy. 'What a place! what a place!' he began to whimper, savagely pushing his hands through his black wild hair. 'What a life, too! To wander up and down from place to place selling nothing, nothing, with nothing to do either but drink, drink, drink. What the devil do you do here, old uncle? How is it that you don't all kill each other in this awful place?' he cried to the innkeeper, who, taking his cigarette from his mouth, merely shrugged his shoulders.

I sat down to a meal of eggs and chunks of sausage, at a seat in the chimney corner. The sight of a strong fire was good. The family gathered round and clawed

at things in a pot, bawling at one another. There
was an argument about selling a mule for three
thousand pesetas. There were six shrieking children
scrambling about the place. Each brother nursed a
child and all watched me like wild animals. At times
the woman gave a shout like the roar of a bull. She
might have been a man.

At ten o'clock her young husband came in,
reddened with dust, fuming with sweat. He had
walked home twelve miles from his work on the
road. He made sounds at his wife and seized the
baby to nurse it with great delight. Every one in
turn took the baby ; they dragged it from one
another and passed it from hand to hand. They
kissed it, threw it up in the air and fondled it until it
cried, and the mother stood watching each one from
the other side of the room, ready to spring if need be.
She began to soften and smile and spoke kindly for
once, but when she saw me she shouted in her old
sullen fashion. More sausage ? More salt ? More
oil ? Wine ? She bawled.

The young husband, with his hair in his eyes and
his voice loose as a stone heap, inquired, ' What ? is
he deaf, this gentleman ? '

Strange and sweet rural delights ! The sheets of the
bed I slept on had not been washed for years, but,
thank heaven, no fleas or bugs came out of the walls
or the mattress. For hours I heard the voices of the
family rumbling and roaring in the next room like a
furnace. From the outside night not a sound. I slept
dreamlessly like a piece of iron flung down. The sun
was well up and flying high like a yellow bird when

I was awakened by a violent battering outside the
door of the inn, till the place began to shake and the
children to start screaming again. At last an inner
latch clicked and some one shouted, ' Who goes ? '
Her voice.

' Men of Peace,' called the strangers.

Peace !

CHAPTER XVII.
SALAMANCA

Salamanca, Salamanca, I whispered to myself, for walking alone one does talk and rave a little to oneself and commune with the sights that stream past, and with the land that lies before one. Solitary for hours and talking to no one, it is as if particles of one's being fell away, as a whispered vapour falls from a cloud, and became at one with the soil and the blue speech of the sky until, little by little, united with the earth, one is less than a shadow or a sound, nothing walking in a dream. Like those gnats flying in shadow that one sees only in the sunlight, a fierce reality shines upon them. It is strange this sensation of unreality, and of the earth's unreality too, that one receives when alone; strange the speculation that but for the presence of one's fellows one might disappear from materiality entirely.

In this moment of abandonment one's mind is like a rain that in passionate squall throws itself upon the earth and air and is absorbed by them. And yet, words went hopping round the brain pan like two hard and constant peas. Salamanca. Then Salamanca-a-a-a, pais blanca-a-a-a, to imitate the austere drawl of those stone breakers hitting the endless stone heaps of that road, hit, hit, smash, left, right, left, right, Salamanca-a-a-a. And the road rising and falling sharply like a flashing baton over cornfields that stood swelling green music like myriad stringed

lutes against the breasts of the hills. Salamanca. Asi
va usted a Salamanca-a-a-a. So you are going to
Salamanca, pais blanca, white country. Like two
peas—left grind, right grind—in the brain pan.
Salamanca, the place was a shrine. That night I must
be in Salamanca, the Ultima Thule, the end of all
things. Salamanca was all desire, it was a god.

I expected great things of Salamanca. Having
walked over two hundred miles for it, I had a right
to expect not only a city, but something indefinably
more. To begin with the anticlimax, the mere
machinery of living, I would find letters in Salamanca. All men are young enough to expect for-
tunes and prophecies and miracles in their poste
restante. The warm chat, the staccato gossip of
letters. They would be wonderful. And they re-
solved themselves in the end into one word that was
happiness, desire, the Ultima Thule and a god—
Salamanca.

But even more of happiness and conquest I expected
of the city. I felt that in Salamanca I should in some
unexplained way breathe of the spirit of Unamuno,
who in these days was exiled from Spain by the un-
utterably stupid dictatorship. The crassest of all
pilgrimages this, walking two hundred miles to find
a man who had been forced out of his country
because he happened to prefer liberty to generals.
' God give thee not peace, but glory,' he writes at
the end of ' The Tragic Sense of Life.' One is always
one's own hero ; if I did not find peace I might at
least blunder into glory.

You laugh at this vague glory. You are amused by

the coming transfiguration. Salamanca, Salamanca, the peas skipped. Yo que soy hombre—I, who am a man, cries Unamuno. Cries, in a man's voice. Not I who am merely the expression of a Mind, not I who am merely the expression of a Soul, not I who am merely a sentient body. But I who am a man. The expression of God that is Mind, and Soul, and Everything.

I do not want a religion in which I send my soul like a shirt to be washed at a reasonable charge and with the minimum of damage from all modernist improvements. I do not want a religion that will pad my jaws with optimism and complacency. As for the biologists, the scientists, utopians, the germ hunters, who tell us all is infinite microscope and serum is its prophet—we asked them for bread long ago and they gave us, by that strange mixture and transformation of metaphor possible only to science, not bread but a tabloid. I regard wistfully the philosophers with their cautious little plumb-lines dipping into the infinite. And in the end I come back to Unamuno's ' hombre de carne y hueso '—man of flesh and bone—to the man who has the kingdom of heaven within him where mind, soul, and body are one. That was the glory of Salamanca. Salamanca, like two peas skipping up and down.

At Salamanca I should rest two days. If only I could get a sight of the city. If it would appear out of the burnt plain. The music of the name brought tears to my eyes. I wanted to shout Salamanca, to sing Salamanca, that dry name with a hundred virile leagues in it. Cold in it, corn and vines and rock and white roads, slow bell-less ox-teams, and miles to the east, Avila, where years before I had first heard the night watchman's hourly shout to the Virgin. Caceres jingled like silver, Plasencia sauntered like its river, and Béjar was less than a spit. But Salamanca was music, a long chord, and wherever my thoughts wandered in the mechanical delirium of the march, left right, left right, of the dumb leaden body, they circled back like a fugue to its theme, ' Salamanca, pais blanca.' White country.

There was something sardonic in that land, and it was not yet white with the singer's corn. Wind and earth loomed ; but in Spain the earth is always rising, rising like a passion storm uncontrollably under the feet, the dust smoking from it, the sun's tambourine of blare shaking it. With the rising of the ground the air became keener and the wind boomed out of the Gredos like a roll of drums to the march. My teeth gritted together in minute tune, a shuddering *marche militaire* gripped and muttered by the jaws. I snapped my jaws again and again on the inward music of the mind. I could have shouted Salamanca, but there was no strength in me. I suppose I had no mind left ; the body went on by itself, by its own nervous habit, as a chicken will walk after its head has been cut off. I caught glimpses of my body speeding on like an overwound machine. This bit of flesh and bones and tweed could never cast itself into Salamanca. It would fall down by the roadside and watch Castile spin round it and lose itself in the music of the lute strings of corn. But it must get to Salamanca and before five o'clock in case there is good news, news

about a fortune, about happiness and luxury and
relief from all care. And there was Unamuno's man
of flesh and bone, that glory. Confound Unamuno,
give me not glory but peace. So I watched my body
grinding into Salamanca over hill and hill, from ridge
to ridge of the treeless furrows, till imperceptibly I
had reached the summit of that tableland over 3500
feet above the sea, where the winds now scalded by
like red steam in spinning dust storm, scratching the
sight as grit will scratch a pane.

I passed through two red villages ploughed into the
earth and at one with it. The places were as empty
as broken pitchers. The chimneys laughed and
roared at me. Only the chimneys in this burned-up,
dried-up place were human and had a sap of smoke
flowing in them.

' By the hand of Felipe Fernandez año 1901,' cried
one chimney, for that was the inscription on it, and
from another this rebuff, sardonic—

> ' Que me miras animal ?
> Soy de yeso, ladrillo y cal.'

> ' Art thou looking at me animal ?
> I'm made of brick, lime, and plaster.'

Salamanca is still turning in my head now I can see
it, twelve miles away, the Cathedral like a hedge of
warriors. I watch it. I grind towards it, the road and
wind devouring me. Down, down, down, the road
is advancing. Nearer the helmets and spears—and
then no nearer. If I walk for years they will never be
nearer. When they seem beyond the next ridge they
are still five miles away. Salamanca, I gasp, I bleed

over the cruellest plain in the world, past Arapiles, where Wellington's wounded groaned ; and now it is very near, yet not so near, and then down the last avenues of thick limes where I can see every window in the city, every tile, every door—which are three miles away. Then I attained it. I descended to the river to see it built yellow terraced out of the Tormes, stippled with sunlight like daffodils.

Possessing Salamanca I desired it no longer. It was now nothing. My exhaustion left me. I walked round the noble Plaza Mayor and felt its gold in my pockets. The crowd stared. I stank. Unamuno's man needed not so much glory as soap. I was happy, and a happy man needs no glory, no religion, no extraneous God, for happiness is God. Eat well, live well, as the Spaniards say. Unamuno could keep his man of flesh and bones. I took my letters into the noisest café I could find. Well cushioned, it scarcely matters if the Absolute should crack across the middle like a plate. And then as I read, my letters were abomination and misery, nothing. The Absolute *had* cracked and the pains of misfortune like a broken spring dug into me. The café stamped itself upon the mind as hard as the stare of clear misery. Cups and saucers glittered and opposing mirrors on the walls threw back recurrences of the same event into each other infinitely. Innumerable cafés, each smaller than the other, in which the same waiters stood, moved the same way, made the same empty gestures, lifted infinite coffee jugs within mirror, within mirror, to the infinitesimal. An electric piano in the café began mechanically thumping the ' Marche Militaire,' like a poor

maddened man marching to nothing. It rubbed and
boiled as though all those tables and mirrors and life
itself were being broken into chiming fragments,
until there was no basis to anything, and all a man
could do was pack his sack again, and march, march,
march—from Salamanca to Zamora, from Zamora
to Leon, Leon to Vigo.

That is what it came down to in the end, the
hombre de carne y hueso, the man of flesh and bones
on a road and the kingdom of heaven within him.

*   *   *   *   *   *

The city of Salamanca, at one time one of the great
University cities of the world, and now a place whose
life has been squeezed dry by the theologians, is the
capital of its province, an ancient city built of yellow
sandstone, and standing like an ornate Quixote in
the desert.

Under the Romans the city became the ninth station
on the highway that ran from Merida to Saragossa.
It was reconquered from the Moors in 1055. The
University was founded. Fighting Geronimo, the
Confessor of the Cid, built the massy romanesque
Cathedral which is called the old Cathedral. The
new Cathedral, florid Gothic and Plateresque, was
begun in 1513. Columbus was laughed at. Lords
and bishops and returning conquistadores drew
yellow stone from the quarries of Villa-franca outside the town, and built themselves mansions like
caskets of gold elaborated with all the precious lacery
of artifice. Here José Churriguera was born in 1660
and held his architectural orgies, more like a pastry-

cook working in some heroic dough than an architect ; and Friar Luis de Leon, imprisoned by an Inquisition, which even to-day finds its apologists and practitioners, mused like a sweet organ :

> ' Qué descansada vida
> la del que huye el mundanal ruido
> y sigue la escondida
> senda por donde han ido
> los pocos sabios que en el mundo han sido.'

Napoleon's retreating French free-thinkers, who had lost their tempers all over Spain, not satisfied with having blown up the towers of the Alhambra and every Alcazar that came in their path, completed the spiritual ravages of the Inquisition by destroying thirteen out of Salamanca's twenty-five convents and twenty out of its twenty-five colleges. The University, which in the fourteenth century numbered 10,000 students, had lost 5000 by the sixteenth, and to-day there are only a few hundred, the youths of the province.

I rested two days in Salamanca, and was lonelier among the crowds than upon the empty roads, where all men are travellers and friends. My entrance into the hotel began humorously enough, but the promising event fizzled out into nothing. I was asked to fill up the usual forms, and for the benefit of foreigners these had been translated into what the proprietor thought was English. The words were :

Proper Name.
Nick Name.
Years.

Rank or State.
Land.

and concluded :

All strangers bearing children under 16 must
    deliver same.

I watched from the cafés the evening paseos, the
crowds in the kingly Plaza Mayor, where within
living memory the bull fights had been held and in
older years the autos de fe. It was remarkable to see
men and women who were not cowed by the stare of
the soil, to hear laughter that was not rough and
earthy.

At ten o'clock on the first evening the ayuntamiento was outlined in white illuminations, and after
the exploding of many rockets and the scorching of
bugles, a procession trailed up from the lower quarter
of the city by the river and passing under the archway into the Plaza Mayor, which was shining like a
polished ball-room, promenaded slowly round it.
The Virgen de los Remedios, like a fairy on a birth-
day cake with candles burning round her in a misty
pretty light, was borne round, the little image
shaking and rattling timidly on its stand and followed
by the terrifying forms of guards, police, and soldiers
in full-dress uniform. The little thing might wring
its tiny hands and weep pearls at seeing the
thousand unreadable eyes of the mystics who were
watching her, a young lady taking her paseo
with the rest. The drums grumped at us ; the
bugles defied us, and the rockets sparked into pop-
ping stars. The doll, standing a trifle askew, looked

fixedly as two blue buttons, and trembling to be back in the doll's house again.

In the morning the sky was low and bulging with dusty draperies of grey cloud. The city was cheerless and boring. Only the Plaza was magnificent, and in it a man was ennobled by the sight of the stone, and in the swing, the down blow of its steep arcades found an aggrandisement of the mind ; but outside the Plaza the streets fell away to strings, and knots, and sandheaps, and a few cold trees. I did not dare to walk far in any direction, fearing to meet that terrible llañura again.

Though at every corner I stood before the wing of some seignorial house, or archway, some blonde façade with the sad lace of the Plateresque upon it, and though there was beauty enough in the city, and struggle and glory, to sustain the devouring spirit of an Unamuno, it is a place that shuts the stranger out, a city whose light is cruel and not tender, an ascetic place without heart or intimacy. I remember standing in one of those cobbled alleys and watching a woman distantly walking towards me slowly along the bit of curb of the endless street. She came so slowly on penurious feet, under that bulging seminary wall, jail wall, so slowly that I, fascinated, watched her wondering how long it would be before she reached me. Like a fly she moved along, head bowed in her black shawl and her face yellow and lined as a convent wall, bright eyes looking out of their prison. How much longer, how much longer. She would never reach me. She was muttering to herself as she passed by.

There were gay things there. A man by the river, a maker of wine-skins, was pumping up a skin with a foot pump—woo-snuff, woo-snuff, woo-snuff—a ridiculous sight to see a calf-skin being blown up by the leg till you evilly hoped it might blow up and split its sides with laughter. To call on the botero and see how his skins were getting on came a woman on a donkey, and she was followed by a man. ' Stop,' she cried, and banging down on to the clay ran to watch the botero. ' Madre mia,' cried the resigned man, spitting across the road, ' women have more fantasies than donkeys.'

The yellow motor diligences, packed with priests, peasants, red soldiers, and luggage, rang their brass bells and jumped out of the town over the river to Alba de Tormes and everywhere else in the province, choked with dust. A man had a barrow of young green snails like unicorns as they pranced and reared from their shells. And the water seller from the spring came by with his mules and cart with vastly waisted jars of fresh water and not the bad, stale stuff of the city.

On the last afternoon it began to rain. Steel rods drove into the ground and raised up fine whistling volleys and thuds of dust from the roads. The rain began to seethe and obliquely drill. I ran for shelter into an archway with an escutcheon and a scroll over it. The house had iron-barred windows. I stood there between the spiking of the rain in an empty street. There was no sound anywhere. Not a voice. Nothing but the steel whistling of the rain. Nothing, as though life were an empty box. As I

stood waiting, an inner door behind me clicked open.
Nothing came out. The door remained a few inches
open and I could see the beginning of a flight of
heavy stairs raised into gloom. As I watched the
stairs, down from the gloom came knocking noises
like a knuckle bone knocking on a door, and then
feet were walking in the gloom and shadows began
to be gathered up and thrown back in new half-lights
on the stairs. Then I heard footsteps light as dulci-
mer hammers on the stairs and saw a small figure—
as it might have been the little Virgen de los Remedios walking about her house—and it descended. The
door opening, there appeared a pale little girl with a
basket, a fairy out of nothing. She left the door open
a few inches more and I could see a heavy balustrade
and the staircase down which she had stepped curving magnificently up like a Napoleonic eagle. The
child looked at the rain for a moment, buttoning her
coat. 'Do you live here?' I asked. 'Si, señor,' said
she, looking frankly at me, I was so odd.

'What is this house called?' I asked, indicating
the escutcheon, the windows, and to turn that
unreal look.

'Es la Casa de las Muertes. The house of the dead.'
She cried pertly, and ran clittering into the funny
rain, a strange man to be afraid of the splishity,
splashaty, sploshoty, silly old rain.

CHAPTER XVIII.
ZAMORA

Forty-two miles of tableland rolled between Salamanca and Zamora. There were combed lines of
corn a foot high and sepia bodies of land, thousands
of acres of it, braided by the plough and pressed
under a sky of chalky, quarried clouds. The scenery
is not magnificent yet it imparts the sensations of
magnificence as though one were treading a wide
cathedral floor.

There were no villages. At a lonely venta called
Los Pozas, because of some wells there, I ate eggs,
fried by a woman with a screaming child in her arms.
Up and down, up and down in the dark little inn,
under its beams, she ran with sticks for the fire, with
oil, with pans, with bellows. In the chimney corner
sat a man who peeled an onion continuously and
watched me. Two more men came in, and there was
an argument about the price of a load of sticks.
Men were cutting the encina in the wilderness which
I was approaching. Twenty-eight pesetas—a man
was a fool if he thought he could get that price. The
woman traipsed about, now giving the breast to the
baby, now draining the soup off the jar of cocido
that was steaming in the ash. They sat down to eat
the cocido, picking out the bits of sausage in it in
their fingers, and first offering it to me ceremoniously,
and I as ceremoniously declining it, in accordance
with the immemorial Spanish formula.

' Le gusta ? '

' Buen provecho.'

The onion man sat watching me all the time, at last he said, ' You might be a Portuguese, but you are not. You might be an Italian, but you are not that. You are not fat enough for a Frenchman. And a Japanese '—his face lit up—' I have seen them in Morocco. They have faces as small as your fists ! No, you must either be an Englishman or a German, because you have a very red face.'

Vast plateaux of floury clouds moved across with blodges of blue between them, a varied and broad sight, westward. The road became sandy yellow and burnt dully with its own heat. Men were cutting down the oak boughs and carting them away in besoming loads. Oak boughs that would burn on cottage fires savourily. Birds sang out like water. A serpent whistled away in two silver twirling wheels into the lavender. I heard flooding sheep bells, and the voice of the telegraph wire boring miles and miles ahead into time.

After twenty miles a sumptuous bus overtook me, and as the inn at El Cubo was filthy—El Cubo de la tierra de Vino—I decided to take this bus to Zamora. It opened its wings like a grey buzzard, spreading them over the roads. How easily we mounted, how voluptuously we descended. Wilderness and hilltop flowed together—how many hard hours would those winged miles have taken me on foot—and then the hills blenched and became flat topped and water hollowed, like skulls with eye cavities staring out of them. We streamed like loud water under poplars

and sycamores. We boomed down dense avenues.
At one village a priest clambered in. He was an
enormous, succulent, and rosy man, smooth as a
cloud, having the benignity of one who ate genially
and well. He saluted me and crossed himself. Then
he began to bite his finger nails. His blunted little
fat fingers flickered blessings as chubby as cherubs
on the bared heads of the peasantry who had come
to see him off. As we mused out of the village there
appeared odd families at turnings and lane corners
and the rosy, bitten cherubs fluttered down among
them.

The sun boiled in and began to ripen his countenance—which could have stood but little more
ripening—so he shaded it with his hat. He unbuttoned his robes. Phew ! I saw his little trousers. So
surprising it is to see a priest's trousers. He was too
polite to ask the other travellers to lower the blind.
I could not reach it either, and the emaciated young
man with a cigar complexion who was sitting by
the window, was hostile to every one and everything.
He snapped at the landscape. He fidgeted his long
legs and twiddled a thin cane with a white dog's
head on it in a way that would drive you mad. You
could hear his tinny breath. The priest got out at the
next village, lowered himself with some difficulty.
He said good-bye in a bland, cloudy voice, somewhat
sculptured, ' Vayan ustedes con Dios, Señores.' The
marble baroque tone of the complete ecclesiastic.
His short blunt fingers flickered cherubs. . . .

The priest was replaced by an enormous woman in
black satin who sincerely thought she was half as big

as she really was. She was shouldered and shored into the bus. She stood up, and lifting up the skirt of her coat revealed a vivid violet lining. I shuddered as I saw that huge block of posterior, that thundery cumulus about to sink its storm upon us. Slowly it bent down, sank upon us like a damp heat against which we could do nothing. She laughed with the raucous good nature of the very large. Ha, ha, ha ! ' How is it they always make these buses so small ? ' she remarked. Every one of her five yellow cushions of chin thudded with dusty and faintly cachou laughter.

Her first gesticulation knocked my hat over my eyes. Her second hit my nose which was breathing covertly below a shady bulge, which I conclude was her shoulder blade. Her arm shot out across my face and she pulled the blind down, saying at the same time, ' Thank you.'

Now we were passing high over the plain in warm flight among those wan table-topped hills in the hollows of which were cupped purple evening shadows. For a few minutes before sundown the pallid tableland, now receding into the valley of the great Duero, the first cleavage in Spain, lay mapped below us, crying with the blenched light shrill as a frightened bird. We saw the white windows of Zamora shining, the vivid evening on its towers and westward houses, and the rest pooled in liquid shadow. Crossing the fishlike Duero we flew climbing round the long wall and entered the town.

Zamora was a fighting city in its day, with the wars of the Castiles scarred on its walls. It belonged definitely to the north, chief city of the corn-bearing land that lies northward to Leon and eastward to Valladolid. In this region the strength of the Moorish tide was thrown, spent, and soon cast back. The history of Zamora lies with the Visigoths, the Romans, and the wars of Castile.

Beneath the walls the Duero is as yellow and green as a serpent, the second river of Spain. Like all the Spanish waters, it is low in the fierce summer when heat saps its strength to the bone, but in the winter it whelms into flood, and with the power of a dragon gnashes whitened jaws on the weirs and swells breast to breast with the bridges.

There was a youth lolling in the dust by the bank of the river watching the fishermen. 'Three years ago,' said he, speaking of the river as though it were a recalcitrant but powerful citizen of the town, 'it rose to the arches, having sunken the islands so that only the tops of the trees were above the water. You could see the rabbits rushing up the trees for safety, the poor creatures.' He was a lazy-faced, orange-complexioned youth, and he wanted only a few flies to be tacked on to his face to make him the complete Arab. 'And what happens here in Zamora?' I asked.

'What happens here? Nothing, nothing. We are very pacific. But we are very religious, too. Oh, very religious. You never saw so many processions as we have. We have almost as many as Seville. It is said we Spaniards are a religious people, but here in Zamora it is a barbarity—es una barbaridad.'

Between Zamora and Salamanca there is a strong

regional rivalry, and by walking through the streets of the two cities I could perceive how Zamora was religious in a way different from Salamanca. Salamanca was glutted with convents, monasteries, churches, seminaries, their little businesses and intrigues, and theological glooms, the friction between the Orders, the suspicions of the laity, all the jealousies of an over-developed and inbred ecclesiasticism. There must have been hundreds of priests and nuns in Salamanca. Zamora had a healthier quota. The streets were not walled with blank convents.

In the early morning I was awakened by the clamour and banging of bells, as though all the cans and pails of the city were being whacked into challenge by the faithful. When one outburst had tired itself, another bombardment began in a further parish, and was taken up turn by turn in the lower parishes by the river. Bang, bang, banging good iron and copper religion that cuffed you on the head and the ears and knocked you into a state of sanctity. I do not blame those Spanish bells, for the Spaniard hears none but the harshest noises, nothing but violence ever penetrates him. Nothing but force ever convinces him. The cruelty of the Inquisition convinced him as it stirred the English up to resist. We must be persuaded by quietness and privacy. Our bells must be sentimental, sweet, and milky. Bang us and we bang back. Bang bells and we have them stopped.

The bells like angry priests were rating the town about the procession of Santa Cruz. You mules and animals and curs get out and follow that procession !

We will make so much row that you *shall* know
about the Santa Cruz. This anvil noise is the voice
of God's Church, iron and copper that made the
heretics jump. This is the great and only Church
because it has the right to make as much noise as it
likes. It is Spain calling God. Even God must be
afraid of Spain.

The procession like a slow black creature, a dragon
with a head of priests and acolytes and an upreared
image of Jesus, aflame with candles, moved on its
belly out of the Church of Santa Cruz and into the
Plaza, coiling about the fierce brigade of American
and Italian cars that daily catapulted down the side
of the cliff out of the city to the railway station. The
speed kings, gods of the accelerator, took off their
caps and watched the mystical creature encircle them.

With its long candles protected by globes from the
pagan winds that blew on to the hill from every
opening of the tableland, the procession was led by
thin old men, each holding a black rod with a silver
crucifix. There is nothing more sinister and terrifying than the mounted, lance-like silver cross, a
weapon to pierce with. An enormously heavy image
of Jesus on the Cross was borne by a dozen swearing, sweating bearers half hidden by draperies
behind a platform. The image was so heavy that it
had to be let down frequently. The figure of Jesus
was carved in wood, an emaciated and suffering thing
—how the Spanish worship suffering and blood—
that brought pity to the eyes. The Spaniard likes
Jesus because he was gashed and bled. For the same
reason he likes bulls. To the Spaniard there is

something ecstatic, mystical in those body gashes, and the ghastly branches of blood congealed about them ; the sense of sacrifice, the refinement of horror, which are so strangely mixed in the Spanish mind with the notion of spirituality. The Spaniard worships blood. ' Mi sangre,' cry the Andalusian mothers, passionately clutching their babies to the breast. The crucifixion is to the Spaniard a higher, transfigured bull fight. That Jesus suffered ; claro, we are so wicked. That he suffered in agony, was bent up, twisted and bruised and broken ; claro, no habia más remedio—it couldn't be helped. That he died ; claro, it was the last brave, ecstatic gesture, the bull's last rush, and the inscrutable matador, the bloodthirsty God of Torquemada, plunged in the sword. Life, the Spaniard finds to be a state of coma in a vacuum, in death a triumph. The blood of one crucifixion is worth to him more than a hundred living Sermons on the Mount.

The pale sun light as oats, shone queerly awry on the hundreds of little silver crosses as they clicked and tapped away over the cobbles, out of the Plaza and into the side alleys, to the drum beat and the break of feet. I followed the procession and eventually stopped outside a theatre where a man was posting up the pink bills of a cinema performance. I asked him were there no plays. He spat into his pail and looked at me seedily. He nodded his head to the procession that had just gone by. ' Entre la iglesia y el cinè—nada. Between the church and the cinema—nothing. With the cinema on Thursday and the church doing something every other day of

the week the people have no emotion or money left
for the theatre.' When I asked him what he thought
of that, he shrugged his shoulders and showed
the truest Spanish indifference, 'It doesn't matter
to me.'

I climbed into the sky to the full height of the city
and saw the Cathedral, somnolent block of ochre
with a beautiful Romanesque doorway, that rosette
of arches rich and sincere. I looked down upon the
tiled roofs caked together, and heard rising from
among them the wheelwright's hammer and the anvil
ring of the smithy. The plains stood upright like an
immense wall with the Duero at the foot of it. How
many times had monks of the Cathedral watched the
dust of the advancing invaders rise in their baked
land of corn and vines and seen the red ravaging fires
built in pillars to heaven ?

There was an old city gate here which was guarded
—for octroi purposes—by a kind old man who had
lost his leg in a cart accident, and because of this his
friends had got together and by this influence and
that had succeeded in getting him the sinecure. He
earned seventeen reales a week, about three shillings.
Fixed and certain it was, and this with the height
above the city walls at which he was perched in
bland authority gave him a serenity, a security, a
breadth of outlook which was like sunshine upon
his face. To sit in the sun and to be sure of
your view and your three shillings! Only the
straggling mule teams, brassy bells slashing as the
poor creatures slid and sprawled with loads of flour
down the hill to the mills on the river bank, and the

priests from the Cathedral above, who always had a
kind word to say, passed that way. There were no
customs. 'Arbitrio,' they called him—it was even
printed in brass on the pink band of his cap—but
who ever brought anything taxable that way?

From this height he could see swinging out in the
river, and seeming to be carried out by the yellow
current, a spit of land on which stood a ruined building with a cross on top of it. I asked what that
building had been, and he said that it had been years
ago a flour mill—every mule team on that twirling
plain bore flour—kept by a company of Friars. 'Ay
yai,' he sighed, for the warmth was like that. 'Those
were the days when the Friars ruled and when they
were the masters,' said he. 'When we worked for
the priests. Now all that is over. It's a wonder they
have not been thrown out of the country. Other
countries have thrown them out. But the trouble
with the priests is that they are too industrious.
They work too hard, and they think too much. They
do everything. They never stop. A priest, one of
those good men from the Cathedral, stopped and
talked to me the other day, as you have, on his way
down for a walk by the river, and a very nice man
he is too, a great friend of mine—oh yes, they are all
very great friends of mine—but too intelligent, too
intelligent—and this priest he said to me, "Do you
know, all the great inventions of the world, the
motor-car, the aeroplane, steam, and telephones and
up to the very wireless itself, were all invented by
priests in the monasteries." "You do everything,"
I told him. The fact is they work for their own

account. Too much. Too much. It is not good for
a man to have as many fingers in the pie as they
have.

'Yet this is a religious city. The most religious city
in Spain. Perhaps in the world. For where else are
there such artistic processions and such beautiful sculp-
tures ? There are figures of Jesus which are marvels,
marvels, and Seville itself cannot touch them. That
same priest told me, "The Christs and the Virgins
of Seville are nothing to those of Zamora," he said.
"Nothing. They may be good and worth seeing,
and the cofradias of Seville may be rich, and there is
no doubt Andalusia is a rich country and an amusing
one too—they are very amusing those Andalusians—
but still," he said, "the most artistic, the rarest, the
most miraculous are the Christs and Virgins of
Zamora." '

A mule team passed, striking fire and volleys of
dust down the hill, brass clashing. The arbitrio
watched it. 'Adios Paco,' shouted the driver.
'Vaya . . .' drowsed the arbitrio, his bright eyes
appearing like berries between the yellow fronds of
cheek.

'But I do not belong to a cofradia,' he confessed,
'though half the town does. There are over a hundred of them in the city. When that priest came by
the other day we were talking about it—just as you
have stopped now to rest a little before going down
to the river—and I said to him, what is the good of
joining a cofradia and paying so much for your subscription when all you get is the privilege of following a procession round the streets, which would be

worth nothing to a one-legged man like me, and when you are dead they give you eight masses for your soul, I said. I said, man, I said, with all due respect to you, when you are dead you are dead, and even if you had five hundred masses and paid for them, you wouldn't be any better off, I said. I said, what's dead is dead, I said to him. " Clearly," he said. Well, said I, I need my eight masses now while I'm alive. When I am dead I shall be in need of nothing, I said. " You're one of these unbelievers," said he. Naturally, Don Pedro, said I, and when we are both dead we shall see about it, eh, both of us ? '

That Spanish anti-clericalism does not deceive me. The Spanish are a deeply mystical and superstitious people. They do not admire the French rationalism. If they speak against the priests, it is more because, as the arbitrio said, the priests have been for centuries the ' amos,' the bosses, the masters, and the Spaniards are feeling the beginning of that world-emotion of revolt against the ' boss.' Religion, as a big and popular movement, does not rouse the passions of the world as much as it used to do ; religious dogmas to-day do not throw us into states of war. No man fights for his religion. He fights for his country, and, as a revolutionary, for his class. It seems that the old dogmas are no longer worth fighting for ; the question is, who shall be the ' amo,' the master, the boss, who shall control the fundamental needs of men, their clothes, their food, their drink.

' Thus,' cried my arbitrio, lifting his closed hand to his mouth and the outstretched palm of the other hand as well, and moving his lips ; ' thus, these are the chief industries of the town—wine and bread. There we have all. All and nothing more. For the rest, to-morrow we shall see.'

He stared at the river and the sun battled on the brassy letters of his cap. He remembered suddenly a piece of news that had been going the rounds these twenty years. 'Man,' he said, 'they are going to dam the Duero one of these days and make electricity. It will be a good thing, because then each man can grind his own corn in his own house.'

Wonderful man. He did not see great mills and factories. The dam would be built so that each man could grind his own corn in his own house. I left him sadly ; the selfishness of men would soon spoil that simple dream of his.

CHAPTER XIX

SHINGLED HAIR

The ballad of the girl who shingled her hair and the man with trousers so wide—as you walked the busy peace of the streets you met it at every corner, men and girls humming it, boys whistling it. It spilled like water in the air, it cried like voices out of the empty doorways and the trees; and the darkness itself was like a haze of music emanating from the earth. The white houses might have been the keys of some magical clavichord. Who shingled her hair and with trousers so wide. . . .

The afternoon had been songless and listless. An exhaustion had settled upon the town. Shops were half-open, half-closed, and people sitting about on benches in the square or in the cafés were almost asleep. After five o'clock when the sun's heat had gone, there arrived out of the warped plains a thin booming of cold wind like a presage of music. People began to move about. A girl who had been writing in the glass balcony of a window went away with her cold pencils. Men who had been playing chess came out of the cafés, yawned. Feeling the wind, they began to walk up and down in lively fashion.

The bootblacks got up from the curbs and began teasing a deaf and dumb bootblack, who stood gaping in an effort to speak his rage, and ended in roaring like a poor animal chained up by something he could not see. But if his tongue could not speak his works could; the very gleam and ecstasy of speech he gave them, rubbed the toes into an eloquence. Soldiers were chattering and following one another about like dogs. Donkeys went by striking their bells, strill strall, strike strill. Nothing was still. And the wind twanging as though Castile were an immense yellow guitar and the grey hands of the moving heavens strumming it.

Presage of music it was, for at this hour two itinerant ballad-singers—a man and a woman—came up the steep hill from the bridge of the Duero between the iron windows—like spectacles on the wise faces of the houses—into the Plaza. The two came up curiously looking at the windows of a town they had never seen before. They had sung their way across three provinces. Zamora—the name had sounded powerful and mysterious in the plains.

The two singers walked round the Plaza and then stopped at the curb opposite the white steps that pend like a row of heavy chins from the corpulent home of the Gobierno Civil. No one took any notice of the strangers. The man and the woman stood watching the people walking up and down like irritated straws. How to capture them? He picked up his guitar. Twang, twing, tweng, snapped the guitar tuning up.

Two or three soldiers turned to stare. One or two bare-footed urchins came very near and stood blinking puzzled eyes at the man's working fingers, which were now rubbing a dry murmur, a scarcely audible monody in the minor, loudening into a sob, lessening into a sigh. Step by step one or two people came across the Plaza watching him, running forward, stopping, running forward, stopping, like cats stalking a singing bird and pretending not to look at him.

He was a short, square man with a head like a box. He wore a cap but no collar, and his chin and throat were a deeply clean violet where he had lately, drastically shaved. His eyes were square, jet and dispassionate, indifferent, odd as two caretakers alone in an empty theatre. He had a thick ink-black moustache. He twanged with the air of a bored bishop strumming his way through an endless prayer. His lips scarcely moved when he talked, but he had a dry toothy way of talking, and when he said something pleasant—though only with an almost secret glitter in his eyes to indicate it—the woman would look strongly up to him and he at her with the most delightful connivance and adoration.

Twang-a-twang-a-twang. A little broken circle of people began to form. You saw by her two pleased eyes that she knew what a dominion there was in music as she tapped her foot in time. Music loosened you, melted you, stirred you deeply like a spoon, picked your money out of your pocket, a penny for a new world. She was a tight little person, small headed and high breasted like a pigeon. Her cheeks were solid apples. She was hatless, and wore a blue coat that was far too small for her, for she shrilled bursting out of it like a bright bud. Her hair was screwed back from her forehead. She stood resolutely taking no notice of the gathering people.

Two nursemaids with frilled spiking starched

aprons crossed over. They wore big silver globes on
their ears like moons. This brought the soldiers
over.

' They are not singing,' scorned a sergeant. ' You
see ! '

The nurses began to giggle, and their laughter
clittered like glass everywhere as they jumped up to
see, over the heads of the soldiers, who was in the
middle of the crowd.

' Ay, what a type of woman,' the nursemaids
exclaimed in the starchiest, spikiest voices.

She took no notice. Only, bird-like, she glanced at
him strumming, ironical as doomsday—the real
Castilian disdain—and for reply there was a white
glint of teeth. It was a slow business getting a
crowd together, but the mutter of the guitar and the
blankness of the man's gaze over the heads of the
people, over the clotted roofs of the town, over the
plains whence he and his woman had travelled, and
her eyes watching the clouds romping like children
among the fields of the wind, held every one. More
than once the sergeant looked round uncomfortably
to see what these two could be looking at. He
became nervous and irritable. Something, what was
it ? The crowd grew, swayed, pressed, and sagged
like a swarm. The singers were walled by breathing,
buzzing faces.

' Ay, they don't sing,' at last cried the sergeant in
disgust. ' Let's go. Do you see how they work, the
old uncles ? '

The woman nodded at the man, and he nodded
back. His fingers began to spring and strike harder.

The couple threw back their heads and stretching
their eyes for the full fright of music shouted their
first song, like Arab singers.

> ' Corred mas que antes
> que sea de noche
>   debemos llegar
>   y volver temprano
> para descansar.'

The instrument crackled in a crescendo storm of
wind. The song rode out of their motionless faces.
From his the dry and brittle Castilian syllables
skirled between the nearly closed teeth. Her voice
was brassy. It rasped like a saw. Over and over again
the same words, the same hypnotising chant. The
rhythm and time possessed the crowd. Every one
tapped feet, jogged shoulders, nodded heads, and
some stood with knowing heads bowed listening
for every word and marking the chorus with an
exclamation.

> ' Lagarteranas somos
>   nacimos todas in Lagartera
>   lindos encajes traemos
> de Lagartera y de Talavera.'

' Bravo ! ' cried the sergeant.

' Bien ! ' cried the soldiers. The peasants and the
soldiers scrambled for copies of the song. Green
copies, yellow, pink, and blue. Lively streamer arms.
In a moment she had sold a score of copies. It was
wonderful. Wasn't it wonderful ? She looked at
him and laughed a laugh that could have been a kiss.
He strummed away continuously, taking no notice.
It was all right to collect a crowd. You must keep it.

They sang their next song and the next happily.
The song of Simon the football player—

> ' Por un chico futbolista
>   estoy loca de cariño
>   y si sigo de esta forma
>   estoy viendo que la diño '—

and another song about a beautiful lady who was
cast into prison for the ' crime of love.'

From her dense little cylinder body the song rose
in yellow bawl and his voice was like a sarcastic
commentary on it.   All the little soldiers were
smiling and laughing and leaning as closely as they
could on one another's shoulders, a ring of excited
mouths. ' Bravo ! ' the garlic shouted from them.

' And now, gentlemen,' said the guitarist, stirred
to speech by his success ; ' now we will oblige the
esteemed public with our greatest success. The most
modern, the funniest song in all Spain, the gypsy
song of the Triana, the ballad of the girl with the
shingled hair.'

' Ay-y-y-y-y,' screamed the nursemaids, feeling the
backs of their necks.

' Anda, hombre,' shouted the soldiers in fits of
laughter at the nursemaids, and slapping one another
on the backs and swearing, according to custom,
by their private parts.

The woman swallowed a laugh. The dominion of
music. No crowd could resist this song. Out it
swirled, spiralling bright notes like rival hurdy-
gurdies. The soldiers were laughing, the nursemaids giggling. How funny it was, getting funnier

and rowdier at every line, until those last devastating
lines, where the girl cries :

' Well, I don't see why I am any more ridiculous in
my shingled hair than you are in your trousers so
baggy that one could drive a hackney carriage and
two full-up tramcars inside them.'

' Ya ! '

' Anda ! '

' Bravo ! '

' Vamos ! '

yelled the crowd in derision. And more private parts.

Then the crowd began to scatter as if the enormity
of the joke had been too much for them. They dispersed darkening the Plaza like a flight of jeering
rooks cawing, cawing. Trousers so wide so that you
could put, what ? Two full-up tramcars and—what ?
A hackney carriage and trousers so wide, man ! The
song flowed like water into the alleys, the yards, the
cracks and crevices of the town, soaked into its
stones, permeated it ; men hummed it, boys whistled
it. The white houses might have been the keys of
some magical clavichord. The two ballad-singers
pulled oranges out of their pockets and began
thumbing the peel about like confetti, in amazement
at the effect of their song.

CHAPTER XX.

CLOUDS

Roads part from Zamora like the flashing of
brilliant swordplay—southward they parry Salamanca, eastward they guard against Valladolid, to
the north cut Palencia, north-westward they thrust at
the mountains of Galicia, due north they lunge
frankly at Astorga and Leon—above all to Leon, for
Leon concerned me and my boots, off which by now
I had worn the irons. Leon was eighty-five miles
away, four days' journey, through country rich with
corn, and hungry villages poor as dirt ; and no inns
in them. Where did the wealth go ? To build those
ugly new buildings in Leon and Valladolid, to fill
the pockets of the ' amo,' the master. The first question at a tavern is, ' what have you brought for
yourself ? ' There is a verse in a song that is sung in
the kingdom of Leon about the harvest :

> ' El gañan en el campo
> De estrella a estrella
> Mientras pasan los amos
> la vida buena.'

' La vida buena '—who did I see passing a good and
comfortable life ? You notice the song says it is the
' amo.'

After a night of luminous rain I rose from Zamora
out of the valley of the Duero, like a ship under a
dirty sky. The land was sad, unnaturally wanly
shining like a sea that is calming down after unrest.

I began to roll with the country, and after I had steamed over the first ridges, Zamora had sunken in a rain-grey blur into the trough of the Duero, and the road was a broad dying red wake behind me. The air was strong, hot one moment, cold the next, swept clean through me, thudding like waves against the iron sides of a ship in monotonous disorder. When will it stop, you shout. The tireless, ever restless land combs on into immense perspectives and immensely far horizons. You move as slowly as the puzzled ship you are, and are wretchedly tired and hot—and yet cold and wettish too, that is the curse of it—before a couple of hours are over.

In these times I looked at the sky. There is breath, and light, and mercy in the dreary ranks of rain clouds flagging low, for the only power that can move them is the freedom of a firm wind, one great freedom liberating the lesser freedoms. How small the little casuists must feel who tell us there is no liberty—because they want to bind us—when they stand in the presence of a great sky.

I felt the wet wind from the west driving up some clouds in noiseless concussions of feathery foam, and polishing others into perfect balls of glass. Other clouds broke and flowed choppily away like a surf in infinite, level perspective till they should spend themselves on the horizon. The air was clear ; and every motion of the earth was audible for leagues ; the cry of a ploughman turning his oxen miles away on the belly of a red ridge, the cries of a woman to her donkey as she bobbed along some sunken trail over the wide land, the jingle of water in a ditch, the

itch of the soil under the prickly blanket of low
cloud, the alarm of a bird. It was empowering, this
dramatic ability to hear a much wider range of
sounds, to read, as it were, the mind and mood of
the earth, sodden and left exhausted, iron-eyed and
moving faintly, speaking for more of that fructifying
rain.

For miles I walked before an inky black cloud that
was pursuing me from the west. There was no
shelter anywhere, not a tree, not a stick, not a beast
or a bank. I hurried on racing that enormous shape
which travelled uncannily over the succeeding ridges
fixing them in a livid glow between daylight and
darkness, and finally smudging them out altogether.
The thing advanced, broadening itself, sliding out
to right and left shafts and spears of darkness that
drilled up the hills in blackening regiments, while
under the main body were hung thundery parallelo-
grams of gloom. I put on speed looking anxiously
for shelter, but there was nothing but distantly two
oxen standing alone bowed to a yoke attendant on
the storm. The quietness and rain glassiness, the
pause of awe, as though the world had ceased to turn
and measurable time had gone out of men's minds.

Now the armies had halted, the squares were drawn
up in indigo masses, there was the scowl of bayonets.
The flesh light had gone from the arms and bodies
of the hills and the road stared with its face upwards
and little grasses gritted their teeth. I stood still
waiting too. Polished armies of vapour, glassy and
ponderous, and out of them like the puff of cannon
smoke parted once a gasp of paler cloud drifting

earthwards into nothing. The edges of the body
were beginning to contract and curl up like claws,
with threat. I waited for the electric, artillery crash
of the rain.

Then a miracle of wind lifted that cloud up bodily
higher and across the country swiftly with its bur-
dens of water unspilled, carried it far away, far and
high and far, with its shadows diminishing rapidly
like the memories of a war. The sun slid out and
under it the land sprang freshly into light like a
myriad flash of arms, league after league appeared
out of nothing till the silvered, hollow hills beyond
the Duero sang out like a music. As the air settled
into its spring clearness, minute villages with silver
towers were picked out by the light and seemed
almost beneath the tips of my fingers, poised like
insects in a brief glitter of life.

    *   *   *   *   *   *

Should I go west to Galicia, should I go north to
Leon? West to Galicia, north to Leon. West
Galicia, north Leon. Leon, Leon, or Galicia.
Galicia, Galicia, Leon, humming to myself. It was
the devil. I could not decide. And the harder I
marched the nearer the forked road came, till at last,
damnation to it, it was in sight. How easy to go
westward. How easy to go northward. When the
ways are easily and plainly marked, it is hard to
decide. O for a sign from heaven !

At the fork there was a woman on a donkey, a
miserable woman in rags, and she was blind, and
with a look in her eyes as though she had come from

another world. Her donkey was led by two little girls. There was no signpost.

'Sir,' cried the woman, 'I am blind. I cannot see the road. These little children do not know, and if we take the wrong road it will be a disaster. The road to Zamora, sir. Tell us the road to Zamora. The terrible thing it is not to have one's sight. . . .'

I indicated the road I was on.

'You are sure. You are sure. And how many leagues is it?'

'Nearly three leagues,' I said.

'God have pity on us. Pity on us. Three leagues, riding so and unable to see,' she moaned. The little children looked up at her frightened, then kicking the donkey in the belly urged the pathetic cavalcade on to the leagues I had left behind me. I discovered then I had turned my back on Galicia and was marching to Leon by the road she had come. The hoof prints of her donkey were on it, following her back and back into her world.

After rain in days of red mud, and red from head to foot in the splashing of it, I fell in with a ploughman returning, and he said, 'Thank God for this rain. It has just saved us.'

'It is all right for you,' I said; 'but it is bad for me.'

'Good for us and bad for you, eh?' said he pleased, as all fatalists are, comforted to find we are all in the same boat.

'We have been praying for rain. There have been masses for rain throughout the province,' said he.

'And I have been praying for it not to rain.'

'There it is,' said he.

'There it is!' said I.

'It's good!' said he.

'It's bad,' said I, swallowing a pint of water from the brim of my hat.

To simplify our intercourse I said I took photographs and sold them when I returned to my country.

'I can see,' said he, 'your trade is like mine. Sow now, reap later. Sow to reap. No reaping without sowing, eh?'

'And without sun, no photographs,' said I.

'But, man,' he cried, 'with a good rain like this, just in time, just in time, the crops are saved.'

'And the photographs ruined,' said I.

'It is what God wishes, no doubt,' said he.

The ploughman and his bedraggled donkey left me, he swearing at it, kicking, grunting at it as it slopped along the boggy road. I was mounted on stilts of mud.

Within the village itself the road went suddenly yellow and dry, for the rain had missed it. The village was a long street of cottages built of sun-baked mud—bricks of clay and straw—wedged into a small ravine. Caves were cut into the side of the hill, and were occupied by gypsies and beasts.

At the Parador, a three-roomed hovel, clean enough and bright with coloured pottery jugs hanging on the walls, an aged woman in rags welcomed me kindly, but asked if I could not walk on to the next village as there was trouble enough in the house and very little food. But I couldn't walk another inch. Groans of women came from the inner room;

and in a third stone-flagged room, a kind of outer
stable leading into the house, a couple of black pigs
were snouting about. I sat in a state of stupor for an
hour, not moving, and listening only to the moaning
inside. Two men trotted up on donkeys, riding
them through the room into the flagged stable.
Three women, pinched and yellow, guttering with
tears like candles and hooded with black woollen
shawls, came out, and the stoutest of the men ran up
to meet them. The stouter man with tears in his eyes
and his big beardy head shaking, began to thump
his breast and sob.

'It is as God wishes. We poor people can do
nothing against His will.'

'Nothing against His will,' responded one woman,
crying to herself.

'Ay, de mi. How hard. How hard,' sobbed the
others.

'Nothing against His will,' continued the man
rhetorically. 'If she lives, she lives. If she dies, well
she dies because it is the will of God. But I came
here to tell you with open heart and in frank and
sincere confession that all I said about her was lies.
It was not true. It is not true now. Before the baby
came we quarrelled, but now we have the child we
are reconciled, and any one who says to the contrary
lies and lies and lies. And now I must go. Courage!
Courage!'

The women looked at him as though his explana-
tion was not worth a pin, because they had known it
all along. He went violently out into the stable,
jumped on to his donkey, and rode away. In a few

minutes a storm of rain that must have overtaken him before he crossed the ridge I had descended by, darkened the inn.

I sat and warmed myself by the fire. At ten o'clock a family dispute began in a cottage opposite. A father was stating that his son had insulted him and the dignity of the house, and must either take back what he had said or clear out. The son refused because, he said, his father knew quite well he was right, but would not for his life admit it.

' I am the master of this house and I would sooner kill you than not be respected,' shouted the father, blazing up in words like a bonfire of furze.

' You are mad,' cried the son. ' You are also beside yourself with temper and ought to cool down.'

The old women shook their heads.

' That family ! They are the fighters of the village. Two or three times a week they hold their scandals in the street. It is always the dignity of the father injured by the independence of the son,' said one in a low, wise voice that surprised me. And when like a fire the quarrel had died down, she said :

' And you want to go to bed ? Have you brought a sack ? '

' No.'

' And your straw ? No straw either ? '

' No.'

They bolted up the doors. They gave me a sack of straw and a piece of tarpaulin, and left me to sleep in the outer stable where the pigs had been grunting.

Under the stable door the wind knifed freezing,

and behind the partition the mules and donkeys were kicking and whinnying, shaking and stinking.

The next morning, moving in step with the mountains of Galicia—serpent back of wind-clear violet Sierra, with the snow picked out on the summits and the sky green as ice above them—I walked into Benavente. Market-day.

CHAPTER XXI

'SE VAN A CERRAR'

I passed the night in Benavente. It is a town built of yellow clay like an Arab village, with a ring of iron-green poplars around it. The town is in ruins, and when the rain falls the little capital of rich, sheep-raising lands becomes like a mud heap. Every piece of beautiful architecture is decaying and rotting beyond hope, pock-marked and putrescent with neglect. The ancient arcades, bent on their cracked and drunken pillars, still give an air of dignity and some character to the town ; but it looks more like a straggling herd of bespattered cattle in a market-place.

I met a man there, a dejected and unshaven person, with that anxious agony of eye and that lined despair of countenance, that intensity of gesticulation—as though he were a dyspeptic eagle pouncing on his own soul and tearing it to pieces in a passionate display of sincerity—with that limpness of body and that vigour of spirit which make the Spaniard. Conversation flaked scrappily and dully from him, like the ash of a dying cigar, until I mentioned I was a writer. At this he glowed with joy, and seizing me with his arm gave me one of those bear-like, chest to chest, back-thumping hugs, the inevitable cry of ' hombre ' uniting us with all the fervour and some of the dust of our combined and exultant masculinities. He also was a writer.

Writing was hell, of course. It was impossible, it

214

was hopeless, it was a calamity, an atrocity, and
a barbarity — nothing more. (Every sentence of
his ended with a violent ' nada mas '—nothing
more.) The Dictatorship was brutal, nothing more.
The country was dying, nothing more. The military
and the censorship were killing everything, nothing
more. He had welcomed the Dictatorship at first in
his paper. The end of the old regime, splendid. No
more war in Morocco, excellent. Lower taxation,
peace, no more labour troubles, heaven on earth,
man—wonderful ! But then came the censorship.
No man could write under a censor. It was a revival
of the Inquisition, nothing more. First you were
allowed a little liberty. They flattered you with it,
nothing more. Oh, they said, in a few weeks it will
all be over. Four years had gone by and it was still
there, nothing more. The longer the military stayed,
the more sensitive they became, couldn't bear the
slightest criticism. You must praise them always.
You must never suggest they are less than the Holy
Ghost. Nothing more. And the result ? Little by
little, the body that is drained of its blood, weakens,
is not that so ? If they drained your blood from you
you could stand it up to a point, but beyond that, no.
O friend, companion, dear colleague, we are suffering, suffering. The spirit withers when the mind is
in chains. Nothing more. But there will come a day.
This cannot last. The Army and the Church are
sowing seeds—man, I dare not contemplate it.

To the inevitable anticlimax : ' This is a rich
country. This is one of the richest provinces in
Spain. There is nothing richer than the lambs' meat

of this land. Here we have lamb chops, man, . . .'
he blew a kiss into the air. Divine lamb chops,
paradisical—nothing more.

The next man I met was full of revolutions. He was
a Portuguese bootblack. I sat in a café with my feet
at his mercy. He told me he had fled from Braganca
after the revolution ruined everything.

'The only thing for Portugal short of union with
Spain,' said he, 'is the return of the monarchy. We
failed a few months ago, but we shall succeed. I am
plotting. Others here are working with me. In La
Coruña there are five thousand of us Portuguese
Royalists plotting secretly to return in force. We
shall return and capture Lisbon in July. We have
made our decision, and it is all very secret.'

'Hardly very secret,' I said.

He took no notice.

'Oporto and then Lisbon, and long live the
monarchy,' he cried, vigorously banging my ankles
with his Royalist's bootbrush. 'Our generals, moreover, are kind and tactful and sympathetic. When
they bombard a city they are very tactful, and people
say, " Even though he has bombarded us, yet he is
very tactful and sympathetic. He has not blown up
our important buildings, nor our wives, nor our
babies. But those of the Republic, they are atrocities.
One cannot think they are men." '

I took the road to Leon, dead straight for twenty-
five miles under an endless avenue of poplar trees.
At noon, as I was approaching a yellow clay village,
I heard an amazing skirling, roaring, screaming noise,
rising from it, though there was no mill, nor factory,

nor workshop to be seen.   Entering between the
close faces of the houses, I found the noise loudened
and roared spasmodically, and there was no doubt
in my mind that although this was a treeless country
there must be a circular saw at work in a mill.   But
coming to the end of the village, all I could see was
an enormous and dilapidated church, with its doors
wide open, and inside a packed congregation of
kneeling men—singing, yelling at God.   That was
my circular saw.

In the evening, maddened by the straightness of
the road and the typewritten poplars, I took a
camino vecinal to Valencia de Don Juan, a town built
on a high cliff above the river Esla, a green, suave
tributary of the Duero.   Within a mile of the town I
had a fellow-traveller in the person of an old castrador, a castrator of animals, who also was walking
to Leon.   He was a humorous, wondering man, but
wideawake in the peasant way.

' I know,' he said, ' what you want is a quiet and
decent place.   No roguery, no trickery, no horseplay,
and a clean bed.   You have to be careful what friends
you make on the road.'

It being tacitly understood that present company
was excepted from these warnings, he began to tell
me the troubles he was carrying with him across the
country.   Did I think his son, who had smuggled
himself out of Mexico into the United States, was
safe from the Mississippi floods ?   And another
worry was about his youngest son.   ' I want him to
follow my profession.   But he must get a veterinary
diploma.   He is excellent in practice—he is clever,

and lacks only an older man's steadiness—but in the
theory he doesn't understand a word. He would
never pass the examination. So I am going to see a
priest in Leon who knows a man who has influence
with the examiner.'

Crossing the massive bridge over the precious Esla,
we went into a tavern kept by a friend of his, and sat
talking with his friend and his wife. He was an
enormous, beardy man, a barrel, with a rough, winy
voice, and very hearty. His wife was an Asturian,
and he was from Leon.

' There is no doubt,' said he with an air of imparti-
ality, ' the people of Leon are the noblest in the
world. The Andalusians have wit and a funny
accent, the Catalans are good business men, the
Asturians,' he indicated his wife who was leaning
on the counter, ' are intelligent. Oh, very intelligent,
I must admit. But it is the people of Leon who have
true nobility, and one could say they are the noblest
people in Spain.'

Mules and donkeys wound up into the town, the
men singing sadly to themselves songs I had heard
in Badajoz.

' I have travelled also,' he said. ' I have been to
Mexico. Half the priests in Valencia de Don Juan
were turned out of Mexico. I went as a stoker to
Vera Cruz. Magnificent country. But it was at the
time of the revolution. I left my ship and went to
stay in a small mountain town where my brother had
a farm, when Pancho Villa's revolutionary army
entered the province and captured the town. They
came up to the farm and pressed my brother and me

into the army. They gave us guns—you ought to
have seen the guns they gave us—we protested we
were Spaniards, and that we had nothing to do with
the politics of the country, but Pancho Villa's men
would not listen. It was no good. Off we went into
the mountains, and for six months were driven from
place to place in running skirmishes towards the
American frontier. Finally, we were hemmed in and
were expecting to be attacked and slaughtered ; any
moment the bombardment might begin. One night
sixteen of us decided we could stand it no longer,
and tried our luck at desertion. We crept out of the
camp, crawling on our stomachs, and at last escaped
over the American frontier. The Americans were
sympathetic. They let us go on to New Orleans, and
there I worked for several months logging pines, but
when Taft ceased to be President of the United
States the job ended, and I returned to Cadiz. Stayed
there six months, and sailed again for Buenos Aires.
There I met my wife,' he concluded benevolently,
indicating the glum volume of woman that was
dumped upon the counter. She smiled grimly. ' He
did well meeting me,' she said.

' Splendid man,' exclaimed the castrador in wonder,
though he must have heard the story a hundred times
before. ' But I do not agree with you when you say
ill things about the priests. There must be some men
who think about God. If they didn't think about
God where should we be ? '

' Quite right,' said the stern woman.

' Let them think about God if they want to,' said
the innkeeper. ' But let them leave the pesetas alone

and let them leave me alone. Not that they've ever harmed me.'

'It's a pity,' said the woman, 'for if they had harmed you you would respect them more. Who would believe in God if He didn't send them trouble ? '

'It's a thing I don't understand, because what about the next world ? ' said the little castrador with puzzled eyes. 'I heard a priest say the other day the world would end on the twenty-sixth of September. Do you believe that, you who have travelled in so many places ? '

The innkeeper glittered, the beading of the brimming wine, 'Astronomers, those who look through telescopes, say the world will end in two million years' time,' he announced.

'Telescopes ?   Two million years ? ' echoed the amazed castrador. 'How much is two million years ? '

'Well—two million years,' said the innkeeper.

'Yes, but two million years —— '

'Well, two million donkeys . . .'   What next !

'Two million . . .' the little castrador's face was wrinkled with wonder and incomprehension. How much was two million ?

'Well, two million mules then, or two million sheep, or two million reales . . .'   The stupid little man.

'Yes, yes, yes,' ached the little castrador, but no nearer the solution. 'But how many *hundreds* is it ? '

'Ah, hundreds ? '   The innkeeper laughed. That was a good one. Of course, how many hundreds ? Let me see. How many hundreds ?

'How many hundreds is it?' he asked me, off-hand.

'Two thousand or twenty thousand,' I said, making calculations. The astonished castrador watched my pencil. The innkeeper stood over me like an impatient employer regarding his clerk.

'Twenty thousand,' I said at last.

'You see, twenty thousand,' said the innkeeper, taking all the credit.

'Ay, twenty thousand hundreds . . .' he narrowed his blue eyes and crinkled his thin face. He was in a great wilderness of country and heard sheep bells, twenty thousand hundreds of them. What a herd. Work enough there for a few lifetimes. Hundred after hundred. How many could you do in a day? the world would last longer than that. 'Yes, yes, yes,' he woke up quickly and relieved. He could be in Leon and get that diploma for his son, anyway. Then again he was afraid. 'But could God live twenty thousand hundred years?'

'Oh yes, He could,' said the woman leaning on the counter.

Bells clanged and smashed their iron. Women filled the Plaza fetching jars of water. The sky was green as ice, and the stars white as little houses. How cold the place was. The inn was white and beautifully clean. No trickery, no roguery, no horse-play, but decent.

The next day I walked into Leon across that bruised Castile, the livid flesh colour of the bitter Zurbaran canvases. But as I approached the city of Leon the plain became more fertile, and there were broad

stretches of trees, and I saw standing out of the plain
the blue snow-fingered forms of the Picos de Europa,
shutting out the north and pending in the air like
faint transfigured palaces of distance. This was the
end of my journey. Three hundred and forty miles
in eighteen days. Not very good going.

I chose the most expensive hotel in Leon, threw
away a lot of dirty clothes, and bought myself new
ones. I ate enormous meals, slept a siesta, sat in
cafés reading newspapers, and longed for the train
that would take me at the ungodly hour of four-thirty
in the morning to Vigo.

I nearly surrendered to the most consuming of the
appetites : the lust for ease of mind—a thing of the
stomach which is the abode of all complacency—
and thereby would have missed the Cathedral. It was
late in the afternoon when, defeating for a moment
the senses, I saw the Cathedral for the first time—how
shall I say—a shell of diamonds caught between two
towers of rock, so precious that in older days men
might have imagined it flashing on the finger of God.

The outside of the Cathedral was ponderous, its
walls solid and blank, heavy Spanish bodies. There
was an earthy joviality in the faces of the prophets,
saints, and Holy Family, good thick Spaniards all of
them, crumbling on their pedestals, as the mystics
do, half-way between matter and spirit. I passed
under the Holy Family, a heavy door on its spring
barked behind me, I stepped into a pit of momentary
darkness, and then found myself treading a clear floor
of stone in a trenchant reservoir of light.

The walls drove up sheer out of the mind's reach

on either side to the wings of vaulting hushed above my head. High in the walls were stretched out the agonised stained windows breaking up the light into a sorrowful murmur of tones. The air was frozen wine, built up of the window colours, coloured ice that penetrated and knocked hard on the bones and picked out every hair on the body. That sharp nave was a dagger stab from a mediæval heaven, a cut to the heart.

This Leon was so Spanish in spirit. Outside you had the heavy cocido walls—the beans, the fat, the spices, the gravy—that is the crude, oily Spanish body; inside you saw the spirit, an exquisite, yearning, knife-like thing, incised with an arabesque of a brilliant beauty and, like an arabesque, leading nowhere, consuming itself with the casuistry of its own design. The sinner goes into this Cathedral, the ecstatic cold knife penetrates him, emotion pours from him like a blood, and he is reborn a Loyola, who, passionately repentant of his adulteries, commits the greatest act of adultery there is by throwing himself into the arms of an anthropomorphic God. Poor mystics.

The naves of all cathedrals are cruel; they are the undeviating spears of the faith aimed eastward with a merciless stroke, an eye for an eye, a tooth for a tooth; the healing is in the transept, that broad human shield of the heart which deflects the merciless theological purpose, with the warm felicities of life.

As I turned to cross before the altar, a small door opened in the aisle and a priest alighted on the floor,

and seeing me called out, ' Se van a cerrar.' Closing.
I had been in the Cathedral two minutes.

I mounted out of the darkness into the animal glare
of day. Children were kicking a football against the
Cathedral door. Under the Holy Family and the
saints and the prophets, the leather thudded. The
corner of the far transept, I discovered, was the
parish dunghill. Outside his shop an idle, floury
baker sat hotly reading his paper. Down the street
wobbled a man learning to ride a bicycle, reeling on
with two friends supporting his nervous progress.
There were old women carrying water-jars and men
trailing in the dust of donkeys : the hot animal
world, the heavy reeking exterior, hiding the
jewelled knife within, the stab of Spain. Se van a
cerrar.

THE END